An Anthology of
Modern Urdu Poetry

جدید اردو شاعری کا انتخاب

Texts and Translations

Chair
English Showalter, Jr.

Series editors

Jane K. Brown	Rachel May
Edward M. Gunn	Margaret F. Rosenthal
Carol S. Maier	Kathleen Ross

The Texts and Translations series was founded in 1991 to provide students and teachers with important texts not readily available or not available at an affordable price and in high-quality translations. The books in the series are intended for students in upper-level undergraduate and graduate courses in national literatures in languages other than English, comparative literature, ethnic studies, area studies, translation studies, women's studies, and gender studies. The Texts and Translations series is overseen by an editorial board composed of specialists in several national literatures and in translation studies.

For a complete listing of titles, see the last pages of this book.

An Anthology of
Modern Urdu Poetry
In English Translation,
with Urdu Text

جدید اردو شاعری کا انتخاب
انگریزی ترجمے کے ساتھ

Edited and translated by
M. A. R. Habib

The Modern Language Association of America
New York 2003

Third printing 2010

MLA and the MODERN LANGUAGE ASSOCIATION are trademarks
owned by the Modern Language Association of America.
For information about obtaining permission to reprint material from
MLA book publications, send your request by mail (see address below),
e-mail (permissions@mla.org), or fax (646 458-0030).

Library of Congress Cataloging-in-Publication Data

An anthology of modern Urdu poetry : in English translation, with
Urdu text = Jadåid Urdåu shåå°iråi kåa intiököhåab, Angrezåi tarjame
ke såath / edited and translated by M. A. R. Habib.
p. cm. — (Texts and translations. ISSN 1079-252X ISSN 1079-2538 ; 12)
Includes bibliographical references and index.
ISBN 978-0-87352-797-2 (pbk.)
1. Urdu poetry—Translations into English.
I. Title: Jadåid Urdåu shåå°iråi kåa intiököhåab, Angrezåi tarjame
ke såath. II. Habib, M. A. R. III. Series.
PK2184.A56 2002
891.4'3917108—dc21   2002040950
Texts and Translations 12
ISSN 1079-252x
ISSN 1079-2538

Permission both to include Urdu poems and to translate them in this
volume has been granted for Faiz Ahmad Faiz, from *Nusqaha-e Wafa*, by
the Caravan Bookhouse (Lahore); for N. M. Rashed, by his daughter
Yasmin Rashed Hassan; for Miraji, from *Kulliyat-e Miraji*, by Jamil Jalibi;
for Akhtar ul-Iman, from *Kulliyat-e Akhtar ul-Iman*, by Mohammad
Mujtaba Khan of Educational Publishing House (New Delhi); for Majid
Amjad, from *Kulliyat-e Majid Amjad*, by Khwaja Muhammad Zakariya;
for Munir Niazi, from *Kulliyat-e Munir Niazi*, by the author; for Saqi
Farooqi, from *Haji-Bhai, Pani-Wallah* and other books, by the author; for
Fahmidah Riaz, by the author; for Kishwar Naheed, by the author; and
for Akbar Hyderabadi, from *Zarron se Sitaron tak*, by the author.

Cover illustration: *Separate Working Things I*, 1993–95, by Shahzia
Sikander. Vegetable color, dry pigment, watercolor, tea on hand-prepared
wasli paper. Used by permission of the artist.

Set in Dante

Published by The Modern Language Association of America
26 Broadway, New York, New York 10004-1789
www.mla.org

For my mother

CONTENTS

Faiz Ahmad Faiz
From *Naqsh-e Faryadi* (Complaining Image)

From *Dast e Saba* (Hand of the Zephyr)

Miraji
From *Kulliyat-e Miraji* (Collected Works)

Akhtar ul-Iman
From *Kulliyat* (Collected Works)

Majid Amjad

Munir Niazi

Saqi Farooqi
From *Haji-Bhai, Pani-Wallah*

Fahmidah Riaz
From *Badan Daridah* (Torn Body)

From *Patthar ki Zaban* (Tongue of Stone)

Kishwar Naheed
From *Be Nam Musafat* (Nameless Space)

Akbar Hyderabadi
From *Zarron se Sitaron tak*
(From Atoms to the Stars)

INTRODUCTION

Urdu poetry, as yet little known in the Western world beyond the horizons of a few specialists, furnishes a glimpse into cultures, religious ideas, and literary styles that, although remote from those in America and Europe, afford significant parallels and historical interconnections. In particular, when one moves into the period of modern Urdu poetry,[1] one enters a world of profound interaction between the mainstreams of Western thought, as expressed through liberalism, individualism, and rationalism, and native literary forms together with their underlying religious and cultural dispositions.

The Urdu language is currently spoken by nearly 250 million Pakistani and Indian Muslims and has one of the richest literatures of all south Asian languages. Urdu arose in the twelfth century when Turko-Mongolian and Afghan Muslims conquered northwest India. It developed through interaction of the Persian and Turkish languages of these invaders with native idioms of northern India. Urdu became the language spoken in the soldiers' camps; in fact, the word *Urdu* is derived from the Turkish word *ordu*, meaning "camp," in which the English word *horde* also has its roots.

Like English, Urdu is an Indo-European language. Just as English integrates elements of Greek, Latin, Anglo-Saxon, and French, so Urdu is a hybrid of Persian, Arabic, and northern Indian dialects. Urdu poetry differs from English verse in that it follows a quantitative metrical system in which meter is measured by the length of syllables rather than by the number of stressed syllables. An even more striking difference is that Urdu is written from right to left, a feature it shares with Arabic and Persian.

Today, Urdu is the national language of Pakistan and also one of the many languages spoken in India. In grammar and in spoken form, it is very similar to Hindi, one of the official languages of India. But Hindi has integrated many Sanskrit words, while Urdu contains many Persian and Arabic words. Further, Hindi is written in a script known as Devanagari, whereas Urdu is written in a modified form of the Arabic script. Urdu is also widely spoken in communities in Europe and America founded by emigrants from the Indian subcontinent; for instance, Urdu is today the second most widely spoken language in Britain.

The modern Urdu poets presented in this book offer a fascinating range of forms and styles as well as a complex commentary on the experience—personal, religious, cultural, and political—of issues and dilemmas of the twentieth century. To appreciate more fully the impact and significance of these writers, one needs to understand certain basic features of the classical Urdu literary traditions from which they ultimately emerged and against which they often reacted. In reviewing the history of Urdu poetry, one also needs to remember that India has been invaded by a number of diverse peoples: Aryans, Turks, Afghans, Portuguese, Mughals, French, and British. Two invasions, those of the Mughals and the British, were critical to the formation and development of Urdu poetry. In 1517 Babur, the first of the Mughal emperors, established his rule in India. The Mughals were Muslims whose language developed into Urdu, as explained above. In 1600 the British formed the East India Company in Bengal, to procure spices, cotton, textiles, saltpeter, and sugar. The British eventually calculated that, given the various sectarian tensions in India and the competition with other imperial powers, it would be cheaper for them to control the whole of India. Various Indian states were annexed, and by 1818 the British had established political hegemony. The way was thus opened for the influx of many Western cultural and political ideas that were reflected in Urdu verse. For convenience, we can divide the history of Urdu language and literature into approximately four periods: an early period, a classical age, a broad modern era, and a specifically modernist phase.

A Historical Overview of Urdu Poetry:
Early and Classical Poetry

In the early period (1200–1700), Urdu began to be cultivated as a literary language in the Deccan area of south India, where it was used alongside Persian, the official language under Mughal rule. This form of Urdu was known as Dakhni. The last great poet to make substantial use of it was Vali (1668–1707?), whose work is considered to mark the beginning of Urdu poetry proper.

The classical period (approximately 1700–1850) began when the literary language and tradition, developed in the south, were adopted in the north. Urdu poetry began to flourish in Delhi and Lucknow. The major poets associated with these literary centers included Sauda (1713?–81), Dard (1721–85), Mir (1722–1810), Zauq (1790–1854), Momin (1800–52), and Ghalib (1797–1869). Ghalib is generally acknowledged to be the greatest Urdu poet and is regarded as marking the transition between the last vestiges of the Mughal empire and the new order under British rule.

Throughout the classical period Urdu poetry retained a close contact, in form and content, with the Persian tradition, in which it has its roots. The formal genres of Urdu poetry were based on Persian models. Three of these genres consisted of long poems, the *qasida*, the *masnavi*, and the *marsiya*. The *qasida* ("ode") was a long poem written in rhyming couplets and was characteristically employed either as a panegyric in praise of the poet's patron or as a satire on people or social conditions. The *masnavi*, of which the most famous example in Persian is the mystical poem by the thirteenth-century poet Rumi, was a long narrative poem in rhyming couplets usually written about legendary lovers of the past or the poet's own experience of love, though it could also be used for religious and philosophical meditation. Some of the longer

poems of modern poets such as N. M. Rashed
might be seen as adaptations of the *masnavi* form.
The *marsiya*, which alone among these long poetic
forms did not derive from Persian, was a poem com-
posed in elaborately rhymed stanzas of six lines each and
was devoted to praise of the prophet Muhammad's
grandson Husain (d. 680), who is viewed as a martyr by
the Shiite community.

The genres of shorter poems include the *qit'a*, the
rubai, and the *ghazal*. Readers of English are perhaps
most familiar with the *rubai* ("quatrain"), as exemplified
in Edward FitzGerald's translation (1859) of the *rubaiyat*,
or quatrains, of Omar Khayyam. The usual rhyme
scheme of the *rubai* was *aaba*. The *qit'a* consisted of a
few couplets usually focused on a theme. By far the most
popular verse form, however, was the *ghazal*, whose ori-
gin extends at least as far back as the Arab poet Abu
Nawas (747–813). Given the literary predominance of
the *ghazal*, it is worth providing a more extended
account of this form.

Ghazal derives from an Arabic word meaning "con-
versation with one's beloved." The form developed cer-
tain strict conventions: it was typically a love poem of up
to thirty couplets, with the rhyme scheme *aa, ba, ca, da*,
and so on, each couplet expressing a complete and iso-
lated thought. The classical *ghazal* was usually written
under aristocratic or courtly patronage and employed
stock elements concerning love and rivalry. Innovation
in the *ghazal* was confined largely to the ingenious and
unusual deployment of these conventional elements and
images by wordplay, extrapolation of meaning, or ironic
juxtaposition. Hence individuality in classical Urdu

poetry represented a freedom to exercise choice only in a given formal framework.

A Western reader may well be struck by the *ghazal*'s apparent lack of unity, by the discreteness of each couplet in thought, emotion, and mood. This feature is tied to the fact that the *ghazal* was written primarily to be read aloud at a gathering of poets known as a *mushaira*, a tradition that still flourishes. The *ghazal*'s design allows the audience to appreciate each couplet in turn, whereas the poem's overall unity might demand study of the written version.

As the Urdu scholar Ralph Russell has stated, the love expressed in the *ghazal* was typically illicit, forbidden by the strict conventions of Mughal society (Russell and Islam 98–99). Perhaps partly in response to the conditions under which they wrote, Urdu poets have long had a tendency toward abstractness: in the *ghazal*, the object of love can be many things—the betrothed or wife of another man, a male youth, or a courtesan. Consorting with courtesans, like homosexuality, was officially frowned on, but it was a part of the society in which poets as well as their patrons moved. In each of these situations the lover knew that his love must ultimately be hopeless, hence some of the stock characters in the *ghazal* were the wretched lover (*ashiq*), the merciless beloved (*mashuq*), the lover's lustful rival (*raqib*), and the cup bearer at the wine party (*saqi*).

Another pervasive feature of the *ghazal*, deriving from its Persian heritage, was the use of Sufi (Islamic mystical) symbolism. In one of his studies of Sufism, A. J. Arberry offers a list of symbols commonly used in Persian mystical verse: *zulf* ("tress"), referring to the revealed omnipotent attributes of God; *sharab* ("wine"), representing ecstatic experience at the revelation of the beloved, destroying the foundations of reason; and *saqi* ("wine or cup bearer"), which stands for Reality as loving to manifest itself through all its revealed forms (113–14). These are just a few of a vast stock of symbols, and it is clear that a central ambiguity lies at the *ghazal's* foundation: the object of love can be either human or divine.

Some of these characteristics are exhibited in the following *ghazal* by Ghalib, who wrote just prior to the impact of the West on Urdu letters (all English translation in this volume are mine, unless otherwise stated):

> Union with our beloved was not in Fate's Design;
> Had we lived longer, we'd still wait endlessly and pine.
>
> We have lived on your promise but in disbelief:
> Had we trusted, would joy not be deadly (though divine)?
>
> Who can see Him, for He is peerless and Unique?
> Were there trace of Otherness, we'd have known its sign.
>
> These plights of Sufism, Ghalib! And this your account!
> A saint we'd think you, were you not given to wine!   (24)

The meaning of the first couplet is very clear on one level. The word for "union" is *wisal*, which refers to both sexual union with a lover and mystic union with God. The second line alludes to the Sufi doctrine of *fana*, which can be translated as "dying to self," a condition of union with God. So the interpretation of this line can be expanded to mean that without a complete death, physical as well as spiritual, one cannot unite with God. Hence this becomes a statement of cynicism with regard to union with God while on earth. The second distich also brings out Ghalib's understanding of the contradictory nature of his faith in both God and his lover. The final couplet involves an additional play on words, such as "wine," in their earthly and divine connotations. One can see here the immense possibilities of irony in the *ghazal*'s form.

Poetic individuality was achieved through form rather than content. Yet the form of the *ghazal* was subversive, almost by definition, on religious and social levels. Though wine and romantic love were strictly forbidden, Urdu and Persian verse abounds with the imagery of wine cup, wine bearer, parties, and boasts about mistresses. This use of illicit imagery was sustained and protected partly by the *ghazal*'s intrinsic duality of reference to an earthly lover and God. But also, in common with the way that many societies have dealt with potentially explosive subversive elements, the *ghazal* provided a relatively harmless arena into which unconventional thoughts and feelings could be channeled and battled out. In the twentieth century the *ghazal*, along with other Indian literary forms, became integrated into a widespread political movement against British rule. In this context, it became a potent weapon of protest.

Twentieth-century poets have continued to write in *ghazal* form, and poets such as Iqbal and Faiz have extended its scope, infusing its structure and symbolism with fresh significance. However, while the *ghazal* has continued to be adapted to contemporary needs and situations, a large part of the impetus of modernism in Urdu verse has been achieved through composition of freer verse forms. The poets included in this anthology have written largely in the form of *nazm*, which simply means "poem" and which can range from self-conscious adaptation of conventional meters to what is called free verse. Unlike the conventional *ghazal*, the *nazm* usually possesses thematic coherence and continuity. Some poets have also written in a form known as *nasri-nazm* or "prose poem," which does not follow or adapt any given poetic meters.

Modern Movements in Urdu Literature

The third period (approximately 1850–1930) comprises what is referred to as modern Urdu literature, though the modernity of this period is quite distinct from twentieth century Urdu modernism. After the poet Ghalib, Urdu letters began to reflect Western influence. Governing the advent of this influence was the replacement, in 1835, of Persian by English as the state language of India. This change gave access, especially through educational institutions, to Western thought. Another factor was the decline of the aristocracy and the growth of the Muslim middle class in the later nineteenth century, a class to which Urdu literature began to cater.

The modern movement in Urdu was begun by the Aligarh school of writers, inspired by the Muslim reformist Sayyed Ahmad Khan (1817–98). Sayyed Ahmad helped modernize the outlook of the conservative Muslim community. He attempted to reconcile Qur'anic teaching with what he considered to be a more westernized scientific and rational approach to knowledge. Another main figure of the Aligarh movement was

Hali (1837–1914), the founder of literary criticism in Urdu; he insisted that poetry be experiential, realistic, and a vehicle for social morality. This modernizing movement culminated in Sir Muhammad Iqbal (1877–1938), who is generally considered to be the greatest Urdu poet of the twentieth century.

Urdu poetry of the twentieth century—including the work of Iqbal and his poetic successors—was forged in the heat of overwhelming political circumstances. These have included the politics of resistance to British rule and the struggle for independence; the partition of India and the creation of the state of Pakistan; the successive dictatorships and instability of this new state; and governmental attitudes in both India and Pakistan toward tradition and religion, especially with regard to issues of individual liberty, class, and the position of women in society.

Ironically, it was precisely the introduction by the British of educational reforms and laws that fostered the influx of Western ideas of liberalism, individual rights, and nationalism, which in turn stimulated the growth of a new westernized middle class in India and provided a basis of the Indian independence movement. In response to various British measures there arose in India two groups—the Indian National Congress and the Muslim League—that were to play a crucial role in the achievement of independence. Eventually, conflict between these groups replaced their original alliance and led to the partition of India, after independence from Britain, according to a geography of religion. Although forty million Muslims remained in India and eight million Hindus remained in Pakistan on partition in 1947, the states were nevertheless conceived on the basis of religious majority: Hindus in India and Muslims in Pakistan. These political events loomed large in Iqbal's thought. Concerned about the plight of modern-day Islam, Iqbal's philosophy attempted to reconcile Eastern and Western thought. After him there arose in the 1930s two broad modern movements. The Progressive Writers' Association, formed in London in 1935, drew up an overtly political manifesto for literature. This manifesto, supporting the Indian independence movement, was broadly Marxist and advocated scientific rationalism as opposed to revivalist tendencies in literature (Sadiq 62). So, whereas Western modernists were moving from realism toward symbolism, the Indian Progressives felt obliged to draw away from symbolism, which had been the essential mode of Urdu poetry (including Iqbal's), and to step into a realistic mode.

Among the leading figures of the Progressive movement was the poet Faiz Ahmad Faiz (1911–84), whose verse shows how traditional symbols can be infused with political content. Although his language tends to be more literal than that of his predecessors, most commentators agree that Faiz, unlike the other Progressives, never sacrificed poetic artistry to propaganda or social protest.

The second modern movement in Urdu literature, led by Rashed (1910–75), developed further this literalization of the language. Under the aegis of an organization formed in 1939 called Halqa-e Arbab-e Zauq (Circle of the Friends of Taste), formal experiments made an impact on Urdu poetry as a whole. What divided the ideals of Halqa from the Progressives was that its members considered themselves to be writing as individuals rather than as adherents to political causes such as socialism. The modernization of Urdu poetry was not merely a superficial matter of writing in vers libre or writing about everyday life. The most profound change in Urdu verse was the relative literalization and desymbolization of the language; it is this that underlay the other advances: the blurring of distinction between poetry and prose, the extension of poetic subject matter to encompass individual experience, a focusing on the present instead of the past, and an attention to detail and continuity of description.

Rashed's earliest poems were written in traditional forms. Around 1932 he started writing free verse in Urdu—some twenty years after the discovery of free verse by European poets. He was influenced both by Arab and Persian writers (such as al-M'arri and Rumi) and by the French symbolists and such Western modernists as T. S. Eliot and Ezra Pound.

Miraji (1912–49) was another modernist poet linked with Rashed and, in fact, won Rashed's admiration as the most remarkable poet of his time. What Rashed valued in Miraji was the profundity of his modernistic outlook, embracing psychoanalytic and French symbolist as well as Indian influences. His poetry is allusive, sensual, symbolic, often written in free verse; it gives uninhibited, sometimes controversial, expression to erotic themes and to unconscious drives and motivations. Miraji was also an astute critic, bringing his modernistic sensibility to bear on his reading of his contemporaries.

After Rashed and Miraji, perhaps the most important practitioner of modernism in Urdu poetry is

Akhtar ul-Iman (1915–). He is known for his everyday themes and use of colloquial language. Like Rashed and Miraji, he was deeply aware of the necessarily international dimensions of modern poetry and of the need for poetry to confront all aspects of real life.

Though the modernism of Rashed, Miraji, and Akhtar ul-Iman espoused the relative autonomy of poetry as an artistic practice and shunned the regimentation of literature by overtly political commitments, they nonetheless expressed in their own way some of the profoundly debilitating psychological and social effects of British rule. They also reacted against many of the prevailing indigenous conventions, both social and religious. The personae in Rashed's poems often express the suppression of the Indian psyche—a psyche torn between past and present, Eastern traditions and Western pragmatism, secular democracy and religious affiliation; a psyche unable to love or to experience an adequate range of emotions. During the Second World War, both Rashed and Faiz entered the Indian army. The poems of Miraji and Akhtar ul-Iman embody an intense alienation; a withdrawal into the rediscovered mysteries of the self; a probing into human subjectivity aided by psychoanalysis, symbolist poetry, and humanistic attitudes.

Given this humanism, the creation of Pakistan did not have for Faiz, Rashed, or Miraji the momentous symbolism it had for Iqbal. Rashed's humanistic sympathies were to a large extent based on his reaction against religious institutions and far outstripped any commitment of his to the new state of Pakistan. The same might be said of Faiz's socialistic humanism, which in fact brought him into conflict not only with British rule but also with the dictatorial regimes of Pakistan, especially that of Ayub Khan.

From its inception in 1947, Pakistan has had a troubled and unstable history, which might be characterized as a persistent conflict between advocates of a liberal democratic state and supporters of a conservative Islamic constitution. Pakistani poets have reacted in widely differing ways to this turbulent political climate. Two further poets in the modernistic trend inaugurated by Rashed and Miraji are Majid Amjad (1914–74) and Munir Niazi (1928–). Their poetry does not bear the trace of political resistance or protest; it retreats, as does the verse of many Western symbolists and modernists, into an intensely subjective world of image, color, and the deeper recesses of perception.

After the work of Faiz and Rashed, some of the most politically resonant and defiant poetry by Pakistani poets has been written by women. The two most important figures here are Fahmidah Riaz (1946–) and Kishwar Naheed (1940–). To understand the nature of their defiance, one needs to review the history of Pakistan in the light of its implications for the status of women. Many women took an active role in the struggle for Indian independence; women were also instrumental in forming the first Pakistani constitution in 1951, which guaranteed all citizens, including women, equality of status and opportunity. Ironically, it was under the dictatorial regime of Ayub Khan that an extremely progressive piece of legislation was passed, in 1961, known as the Family Law Ordinance. This law discouraged polygamy, legal under Islamic law, and attempted to regulate divorce procedures. In 1973 a new constitution was drafted, which guaranteed women equal access to and protection by the law. It also granted universal suffrage. But in the late 1970s this liberal trend was reversed by a notorious item of legislation known as the Hudood Ordinance, which covered issues such as rape, fornication, adultery, and prostitution. The effect of the ordinance was to promote a mood of traditionalism and even to encourage the harassment of women; in fact, violence against women increased. The Hudood Ordinance provoked reaction from women's groups such as Women's Action, and since that time a number of women writers and poets have braved scorn, threats, and even violence to make their defiant voices heard.

Riaz's verse is pervasively concerned with the notion of voice. In the preface to her volume *Patthar ki Zaban* (1967, 1975; Tongue of Stone), she aligns the voice of stone with the contemporary plight of women. The next generation of women, she observes, will have greater knowledge and fortitude: through it, the stone's voice will "soften" (11–12). In the preface to her *Badan Daridah* (1998; Torn Body), she observes that some have objected to the alleged obscenity and sensationalism in her book. Her rejoinder is that essentially a poet talks to herself and that the audience does not impinge on the act of creation. She speaks of the courage needed to liberate one's true voice when one is in conflict with both shattered traditions and conventional—often religious—modes of coping with a wrecked inheritance. Artists, she states, bang their heads on the wall of social and artistic conventions: the heads break, but so does the wall, which is hollow. She ends her preface with characteristic defiance: "These poems I will read loudly. If people are shocked, what of it?" (7–9).

Another female poet who has effectively challenged conventional male assumptions about women is Naheed. During her editorship of the prestigious journal *Mah-e Nau*, she was charged with a multitude of offenses, including obscenity for publishing an abridged form of Simone de Beauvoir's *The Second Sex*. Along with Riaz, Naheed has been a pioneer in giving expression to women's dilemmas and perspectives.

It is worth remembering that the traditions of Urdu poetry thrive not only in the Indian subcontinent but also in emigrant communities in other countries. There is, for example, a large literary Urdu community in London and other parts of England; to this day it attends large public poetic gatherings *(mushaire)* and produces verse in many forms, ranging from the *ghazal* through various kinds of *nazm*. While there are many fine poets in these emigrant communities, I am including in this book the two whose verse is best known to me. The first is Saqi Farooqi, one of the most powerful voices in Urdu poetry today. His stylistic iconoclasm and originality of content have made a considerable impact on the world of Pakistani letters. Farooqi is an example of a poet who, living in the West, has attempted to reinvigorate modern Urdu verse through the introduction of innovative techniques and attitudes. The second is Akbar Hyderabadi, in whose work the beauty of romantic expression has persisted alongside modern dispositions.

Both collectively and individually, these poets have contributed to Urdu poetry and the world of literature in general. What fundamentally separates their

modernism from that of Iqbal, whose work is not
included in this volume, is that Iqbal's vision was essen-
tially and profoundly religious and largely expressed in
traditional forms. What unifies the poets in this volume
is that their vision has been secular and humanistic in its
revisiting of religious values and traditions in the prob-
lematic light of modern social and political contexts.
They have probed deeply not only social issues such as
class, the status of women, and imperial domination but
also individual freedom, identity, and purpose. They
have probed the very apparatus of human perception,
sensation, and emotion as these engage the world of the
twentieth century. In literary terms, the modernism of
these poets exhibits a unique blend of traditional ele-
ments and modes—derived from previous Urdu, Arabic,
and Persian literary conventions as well as from local
Indian dialects—with modern dispositions adapted in
part from Western writers. The shift from an essentially
symbolic mode to a more realistic and literal mode of
thought and writing has meant the profoundest change
of outlook and style. Nonetheless, this new modernism
often differs considerably from its counterparts in
Western traditions. For one thing, much Urdu poetry,
like Faiz's, retains a deeply symbolic basis, although the
symbolic content is much altered. Even Urdu poetry that
treats of actual social and psychological dilemmas tends
to be far more abstract than modern Western poetry.
The realism in Urdu verse is thematic insofar as it repre-
sents a new attention to things of this world rather than
to a spiritual or divine realm; it also exhibits a frequent
focus on individual psychology and perception; but it is
often not marked by the elements that characterize

Western literary realism: accumulation of detail, specificity of setting, and narrative development along lines of probability and causality.

The poems presented here retain many images and themes from previous traditions of Urdu poetry. In Faiz, we find the rose garden, the nightingale, spring, the dawn breeze, and wine. The rose garden, which once might have signified a paradisal state or the bliss of union with one's beloved, might now signify political equality or freedom from imperial oppression. The dawn breeze might be freedom, and wine might stand for political or psychological truth as opposed to its traditional symbolism of divine revelation or religious intoxication. The poetry of Rashed, Miraji, Akhtar ul-Iman, Majid Amjad, Munir Niazi, and Akbar Hyderabadi is replete with images of lamp, mirror, traveler, night, morning, mountain, sea, desert, and garden. In the work of these poets, such images take their significance from their situation in the verbal texture of the poem; but this literal and contextual meaning is inevitably strained through layers of symbolic significance accumulated by a word or phrase over centuries. The poetry of Riaz is marked by sensuous imagery, immediacy of situation, and a flouting of religious convention. Naheed's verse often takes the form of a realistic narrative with accumulated detail in a distinctly individual tone. Farooqi's poetry is well-known for its chiseled and precise imagery that attempts to undermine tradition in both attitude and style. Most of these writers have experimented with free verse, which in Urdu tends to be written in regular meter with lines of varying length. Overall, these poets offer a glimpse into the deeper psyche of the Indian subcontinent and its troubled journey through the course of the last century.

Finally, it should be said that the poets in this volume represent merely a selection of the major modern trends in Urdu poetry after Iqbal. Beyond them, numerous other voices have made rich and often pioneering contributions to the development of Urdu poetry. Some important figures who for reasons of space do not appear in this volume are Ali Sardar J'affari and Kaifi Azmi, leading figures in the Progressive Writers movement; the extremely popular poets Ahmad Firaz and Habib Jalib; Amiq Hanafi, a pioneer in the tradition of Rashed; and Iftikhar Arif, a poet with a rich range of themes and forms. To include them and to do them justice would have required a much larger book.

I should like to thank the following people whom I interviewed: Sheila Rashed, Faiz Ahmad Faiz, Alys Faiz, Akhtar ul-Iman, Shamsur Rahman Farooqi, Fahmidah Riaz, Kishwar Naheed, and Dr. Mughni Tabassum. I appreciate warmly the permissions granted by the following people to reprint the Urdu texts in this volume: Ahmad Najib of the Caravan Book House, Lahore; N. M. Rashed's daughter, Yasmin Hassan; Dr. Jamil Jalibi; Akhtar ul-Iman; Munir Niazi; Dr. Khwaja Muhammad Zakariya; Saqi Farooqi; Fahmidah Riaz; Kishwar Naheed; and Akbar Hyderabadi. I am also indebted to Saqi Farooqi for the benefit of his expertise, to Akbar Hyderabadi for his rich insights, and to Dr. Jamil Jalibi for his generous help and advice. Phyllis Triestman of Rutgers University helped generously in assembling this manuscript. I am grateful to Martha Evans of the MLA for her meticulous handling of this project and to

Michael Kandel of the MLA for his meticulous copy-editing. Lastly, I would like to record my gratitude to my wife, Yasmeen, and my mother, Siddiqua Shabnam, for their ever gracious help and support, and to my children, Hishaam and Hasan, for embodying a poetry I cannot translate.

Note

[1]The word *modern* is used here to refer broadly to the period from the early nineteenth century onward. The word *modernist* refers specifically to poets like Rashed and Miraji who share significant parallels of technique and outlook with twentieth-century Western modernists such as T. S. Eliot and Ezra Pound, whose verse appeared largely between 1910 and 1930.

Works Cited

Arberry, A. J. *Sufism: An Account of the Mystics of Islam.* London: Allen, 1963.

Ghalib, Mirza Asadullah Khan. *Diwan-e Ghalib* (Collected Works of Ghalib). Karachi: Fazli, 1997.

Riaz, Fahmidah. *Badan Daridah* (Torn Body). Karachi: Pakistani Adab, 1998.

———. *Patthar ki Zaban* (Tongue of Stone). Karachi: Maktaba e Danial, 1981.

Russell, Ralph, and Khurshidul Islam. *Three Mughal Poets: Mir, Sauda, Mir Hasan.* London: Allen, 1969.

Sadiq, Muhammad. *Twentieth-Century Urdu Literature.* Bombay: Padmaja, 1947.

SUGGESTIONS FOR FURTHER READING

Arberry, A. J. *Sufism: An Account of the Mystics of Islam.* London: Allen, 1963.

Iqbal, Mohammad. *The Reconstruction of Religious Thought in Islam.* New Delhi: Kitab Bhavan, 1984. This series of lectures provides a profound insight into Iqbal's thought.

Kiernan, Victor. *Poems by Faiz.* London: Allen, 1971. Contains an excellent detailed introduction to Faiz and his work.

Matthews, D. J. *Iqbal: A Selection of the Urdu Verse: Text and Translation.* London: School of Oriental and African Studies, 1993. An extremely useful selection, with detailed notes and an introduction.

Matthews, D. J., and Christopher Shackle. *An Anthology of Classical Urdu Love Lyrics: Texts and Translations.* London: Oxford UP, 1972. Extremely useful for those wishing to explore classical Urdu poetry further.

Matthews, D. J., Christopher Shackle, and Shahrukh Husain. *Urdu Literature.* London: Urdu Markaz, 1985. A concise and very readable account of Urdu literature from its beginnings to the modern period.

Pritchett, Frances. *Nets of Awareness: Urdu Poetry and Its Critics.* Karachi: Oxford UP, 1995. An extremely insightful reevaluation of the *ghazal* in its historical and political contexts.

Ratan, Jai, ed. *Contemporary Urdu Short Stories: An Anthology.* Bangalore: Sterling, 1991. A fascinating introduction to Urdu fiction in English translation.

Russell, Ralph, ed. *Ghalib: The Poet and His Age*. London: Allen, 1972. A rich selection of essays on the life, poetry, and historical context of the greatest Urdu poet.

Russell, Ralph, and Khurshidul Islam. *Three Mughal Poets: Mir, Sauda, Mir Hasan*. London: Allen, 1969. An excellent account.

Sadiq, Muhammad. *A History of Urdu Literature*. London: Oxford UP, 1964. An excellent comprehensive study that effectively ends with Iqbal's literary generation.

———. *Twentieth-Century Urdu Literature: A Review*. Bombay: Padma, 1947. Though dated, this account is still readable, and its treatment includes most of the authors in *Modern Urdu Poetry*.

Singh, Iqbal. *The Ardent Pilgrim: An Introduction to the Life and Work of Mohammed Iqbal*. Delhi: Oxford UP, 1997. A highly acclaimed study.

Singh, Khushwant. *Muhammad Iqbal: Shikwa and Jawab-e Shikwa: Complaint and Answer: Iqbal's Dialogue with Allah*. Delhi: Oxford UP, 1981. An English rendering of Iqbal's great poem, with an introduction.

PRINCIPLES OF TRANSLATION

My first aim as translator has been to achieve a balance between an accurate rendering of a poem and a translation that might have some value as an English poem. I have sometimes sacrificed literal accuracy in favor of an accuracy of mood, atmosphere, or tone. Renderings that are overly literal often strike an American or British reader as uninteresting or even banal. They may well defeat the purpose of translation, which at the most basic level must be to convey something of the imaginative power, formal beauty, and connotative richness of the original. The translation itself must be enjoyable so as to awaken the reader's desire to learn more about the tradition and context of the original work.

Hence, in my view, the accuracy of a translation must be grounded in principles deeper than the imperative toward a localized verbal accuracy, which operates merely on a word-for-word or phrase-for-phrase basis. Such principles include the consideration of how particular words and phrases contribute to the effect and significance of the poem as a whole and an awareness of the place a poem occupies not only in a given writer's canon but also in the overall tradition to which that writer belongs. The writer, for example, may be invoking a conventional image in earnest or to subvert it. Consequently an intimate knowledge is needed of writers' original aims, of how they saw their work as intervening in their literary milieux. My own knowledge of the poets in this anthology is not entirely secondhand or gained through published material. I have met Faiz and interviewed both him and his wife; I have talked extensively with Rashed's widow, Sheila Rashed; I have interviewed Kishwar Naheed in Pakistan as well as Miraji's close friend Akhtar ul-Iman in Bombay. While I certainly do not believe that any author's self-assessment is unquestionably authoritative, I do think that intimate access to an author's mind (e.g., through interviews and unpublished material) furnishes a solid basis for subsequent inquiry, interpretation, and a translation that is faithful to the spirit of the original. It needs also to be said that most modern poetry written in Urdu has very little punctuation; I have added punctuation only where it is necessary to convey the original syntax. An example of my approach is the first line of Rashed's poem "Near the Window." A literal translation of it might read:

Awake, candle of the bedchamber of union . . . !

The problem with this rendering (apart from its obvious clumsiness of meter and image) is that its connotative force is lost on an American or English reader unaware of its romantic and mystical significance. The Urdu (originally Arabic) word for "candle" is conventionally used in conjunction with "moth": the candle signifies the beloved toward whom the moth is drawn in helpless distraction. Yet this association does not accrue to the English word *candle*. Again, the Urdu word for "union" (derived from Persian) can signify both sexual intercourse and mystical union with God: this association, too, is lost in English. In the search for English equivalents, it would be a mistake to translate the line into a colloquial idiom; the deliberate archaism must be retained since the original diction is Persianized and locates itself consciously in a classical tradition of love poetry. Only against this stylized opening can the poem's subsequent colloquialism, signaling its subversion of that tradition, effectively flower. I have rendered the line as

Lamp of Love's chamber, awake!

This translation substitutes for "union" the word "love," which in English can invoke both personal and theological (including mystical) registers; it retains an alliteration ("lamp" and "love") that punctuates the original; it seeks to preserve something of the original metrical flow by commencing with a trochee rather than an iamb or a spondee. Moreover, "love" is capitalized to express the general tradition of love in which this poem's love is situated instead of referring initially to a specific love. Finally, the word "chamber," as used here, is an archaism. In this way, assessment of a poem's relation to preceding tradition influences the choice of diction and syntax.

Later in the poem Rashed uses a different word for "candle," in a line I have translated as

The tiny lantern of Self flickers . . .

The translator's problem here is to allude to the poem's initial image of a lamp without precisely echoing it. "Lantern" both alliteratively and imagistically recalls the first line. The themes and import of the entire poem come into play in the translator's decision on an appropriate word: the first line is literally arousing from its slumbers a tradition reposing in classical convention; the line just quoted alludes to what Iqbal saw as a repression of the self, of individuality, in the Muslim world. In Rashed's poem, the two tendencies are seen as concomitant, which is why "lamp" and "candle" reverberate in both contexts. It is clear also that the choice of diction and phrasing here must be informed by our knowledge that Rashed himself attempted to promote individualism as both a political and a literary ideal.

The poem "Desolate Sheba," also by Rashed, presents a rich example of intercultural symbolism. The figure of Solomon is used as a metaphor for modern dictators who bring about their own and others' ruin:

Solomon, head in his hands, and Sheba desolate,
Sheba desolate, the home of ghosts,
Sheba an endless heap of woes,
World devoid of grass, greenery, and flower,
Winds thirsty for rain,
Birds of the desert, beaks tucked beneath their wing
And men, choked on dust.
Solomon, head in his hands, bitterly disheveled hair,

World-dominion, world-administration, merely the
   bounding of a deer;
Love a leaping flame, lust the odor of odorless flowers:
Speak less of the age's mysteries!

Rashed's portrayal of Solomon draws on the complex
symbolism of Solomon in both the Qur'an and the
Old Testament. Solomon, son of David and king of
Israel from c. 970 BC, is repeatedly associated in the Old
Testament with wealth and wisdom, as in this extract:
"So King Solomon exceeded all the Kings of the earth for
riches and for wisdom" (1 Kings 10.23). He was visited
by the queen of Sheba (called Bilqis in Arabic tradition),
who acknowledged his wisdom and his favor in the sight
of God (10.7–10). But later Solomon is said to do "evil in
the sight of the Lord" (11.6).

In the Qur'an, Solomon is said to have been given
knowledge by God (27.15) as well as power over the
wind (34.12). Sheba, a city in Yemen, is described in the
Qur'an as a beautiful gardened terrain, sustained by a
dam that made it a prosperous and civilized area until its
people turned away from God; the dam was destroyed
and this flourishing "Garden of Arabia" was turned into
a wasteland (340.15–16). This destruction is the starting
point of Rashed's poem.

Specific images in the poem reflect details of scrip-
tural and Qur'anic accounts of Solomon. The "Winds
thirsty for rain" could carry a significance derived from
the Qur'an. As well as reiterating the traditional life-
giving associations of rain, the Qur'an ascribes various
symbolisms to the winds: they are heralds of "glad
tidings," purifying agencies (30.46–48) and renewers of

life (70.57). The "bounding of a deer" is reminiscent of
the Song of Solomon in the Old Testament: "The voice
of my beloved! behold, he cometh leaping upon the
mountains, skipping upon the hills. My beloved is like
a roe or a young hart" (2.8–9). The "leaping flame"
may echo an image in a love sonnet by Stéphane
Mallarmé (whom Rashed had read): *La chevelure, vol
d'une flamme* [. . .] (Her hair, a leaping flame [. . .]).
Finally, the line "Speak less of the age's mysteries!"
recalls a verse from the Persian poet Hafez:

> Engage less oft in mysteries of things [. . .]
> Indulge more oft in love and song and wine [. . .]
>   (Nakosteen 167)

Throughout, I have attempted to render the Urdu
lines and phrases such that they retain the original mean-
ing while connoting the echoes of the various sources
of symbolism such as the Old Testament, the Qur'an,
Mallarmé, and Hafez. This approach seems to make for
a richer reading of the poem, one that broadens the
poem's contexts to include both Eastern and Western
traditions of thought and literature.

I should acknowledge, finally, that all translations are
interpretations of an original, and mine express the
viewpoint of only one interpreter. Whether or not they
are successful is, as always, for the reader to judge.

Work Cited

Nakosteen, Mehdi, trans. *The Ghazaliyyat of Haafez of Shiraz.*
  Boulder: Este Es, 1973.

PRIMARY TEXTS

Akhtar ul-Iman. *Sar o Saman* (Belongings). Bombay: Rakhshandah Kitab Ghar, 1983.

Amjad, Majid. *Kulliyat-e Majid Amjad* (Collected Works). Lahore: Mawara, n.d.

Faiz Ahmad Faiz. *Nusqaha-e Wafa: Mukammal Majmu'a-e Kalam* (Prescription of Faithfulness: Complete Works). Maktaba Karwan, n.d.

    Dast-e Saba (107–90)
    Dast-e Tah-e Sang (311–69)
    Naqsh-e Faryadi (13–96)
    Zindan Namah (235–90)

Farooqi, Saqi. *Haji-Bhai, Pani-Wallah*. London: Highgate Poets, 1996.

Hyderabadi, Akbar. *Zarron se Sitaron tak* (From Atoms to the Stars). Lahore: Sang e Mil, 1993.

Miraji. *Kulliyat-e Miraji* (Collected Works). Ed. Jamil Jalibi. Lahore: Sang e Mil, 1996.

Naheed, Kishwar. *Be Nam Musafat* (Nameless Space). Lahore: Sang e Mil, 1991.

Niazi, Munir. *Kulliyat-e Munir Niazi* (Collected Works). Lahore: Mawara, 1993.

Rashed, N. M. *Iran men Ajnabi* (Foreigner in Iran). 1955. Lahore: Munir Niazi, 1969.

———. *La = Insan* (X = Man). Lahore: Munir Niazi, 1969.

————. *Mawara* (Beyond). 1941. Lahore: Munir Niazi, 1969.

Riaz, Fahmidah. *Badan Daridah* (Torn Body). Karachi: Pakistani Adab, 1998.

————. *Patthar ki Zaban* (Tongue of Stone). Karachi: Maktaba-e Danial, 1981.

An Anthology of
Modern Urdu Poetry

جدید اردو شاعری کا انتخاب

Faiz Ahmad Faiz

Faiz Ahmad Faiz (1911–84) was born in Sialkot, Pakistan. After obtaining his MA from Punjab University in Lahore in 1934, he became a lecturer in English. During the Second World War he joined the Indian army and eventually became a member of the Order of the British Empire. He edited the *Pakistan Times* and worked abroad for various left-wing publications. Committed to political activism, he was jailed by the British for conspiracy. He was also jailed by the Pakistani government for expressing his political views. He received a number of awards for his poetry, including the Lenin Peace Prize in 1970. His popularity as a poet has been vast. While writing for the most part in traditional meters and rhythms, he used the *ghazal* and other traditional forms to new effect, blending Romanticism and realism. His verse tends to infuse conventional symbols, such as wine, rose, nightingale and wine bearer with a new, political significance. Notwithstanding his left-wing political stance, his verse never sacrifices poetic technique for the sake of mere propaganda.

اشعار

رات یوں دل میں تری کھوئی ہوئی یاد آئی
جیسے ویرانے میں چپکے سے بہار آجائے
جیسے صحراؤں میں ہولے سے چلے بادِ نسیم
جیسے بیمار کو بے وجہ قرار آجائے

مجھ سے پہلی سی محبّت مری محبوب نہ مانگ

مجھ سے پہلی سی محبّت مری محبوب نہ مانگ
میں نے سمجھا تھا کہ تو ہے تو درخشاں ہے حیات
تیرا غم ہے تو غمِ دہر کا جھگڑا کیا ہے
تیری صورت سے ہے عالم میں بہاروں کو ثبات
تیری آنکھوں کے سوا دنیا میں رکھّا کیا ہے؟
تو جو مِل جائے تو تقدیر نِگوں ہو جائے
یوں نہ تھا، میں نے فقط چاہا تھا یوں ہو جائے
اور بھی دُکھ ہیں زمانے میں محبّت کے سوا
راحتیں اور بھی ہیں وصل کی راحت کے سوا
اَن گنت صدیوں کے تاریک بہیمانہ طلسم
ریشم و اطلس و کمخواب میں بُنوائے ہوئے
جا بجا بکتے ہوئے کوچہ و بازار میں جِسم

FROM *Naqsh-e Faryadi*
(**Complaining Image**)

Verses

In the night your lost memory returned to my heart

Like Spring sliding softly over barrenness,

Like the slow zephyr gliding over a desert,

Like peace falling, by chance, over a sick man.

Do Not Ask, My Love, for the Love We Had Before

Do not ask, my love, for the love we had before:

You existed, I told myself, so all existence shone,

Grief for me was you; the world's grief was far.

Spring was ever renewed in your face:

Beyond your eyes, what could the world hold?

Had I won you, Fate's head would hang, defeated.

Yet all this was not so, I merely wished it so.

The world knows sorrows other than those of love,

Pleasures beyond those of romance:

The dread dark spell of countless centuries

Woven with silk and satin and gold brocade,

Bodies sold everywhere, in streets and markets,

خاک میں لتھڑے ہوئے خون میں نہلائے ہوئے

لوٹ جاتی ہے ادھر کو بھی نظر کیا کیجئے

اب بھی دلکش ہے ترا حسن، مگر کیا کیجئے

اور بھی دکھ ہیں زمانے میں محبّت کے سوا

راحتیں اور بھی ہیں وصل کی راحت کے سوا

مجھ سے پہلی سی محبّت مری محبوب نہ مانگ

تنہائی

پھر کوئی آیا دلِ زار، نہیں کوئی نہیں

راہرو ہوگا، کہیں اور چلا جائے گا

ڈھل چکی رات، بکھرنے لگا تاروں کا غبار

لڑکھڑانے لگے ایوانوں میں خوابیدہ چراغ

سوگئی راستہ تک تک کے ہر اک راہگزار

اجنبی خاک نے دھندلا دیے قدموں کے سُراغ

گل کرو شمعیں، بڑھا دو مَے و مینا و ایاغ

اپنے بے خواب کواڑوں کو مقفّل کرلو

اب یہاں کوئی نہیں، کوئی نہیں آئے گا

Besmeared with dirt, bathed in blood,

Crawling from infested ovens,

Pus oozing from rotting ulcers:

My gaze returns to these: what can I do?

Your beauty still haunts me: what can I do?

The world is burdened by sorrows beyond love,

By pleasures beyond romance,

Do not demand that love which can be no more.

Loneliness

Someone has come, sad heart. Alas, no one!

A traveler it must be, bound elsewhere.

Night is dying and the starry mist scatters;

In the halls, sleepy lanterns begin to sputter;

Every road, weary with waiting, is asleep.

Foreign soil has hidden all footprints.

Snuff the candles, take away wine, flask, and cup!

Lock up your sleepless gates.

No one will come now, no one.

چند روز اور مری جان!

چند روز اور مری جان! فقط چند ہی روز

ظلم کی چھاؤں میں دم لینے پہ مجبُور ہیں ہم

اور کچھ دیر ستم سہ لیں، تڑپ لیں، رو لیں

اپنے اجداد کی میراث ہے معذور ہیں ہم

جسم پر قید ہے، جذبات پہ زنجیریں ہیں

فکر محبوس ہے، گفتار پہ تعزیریں ہیں

اپنی ہمّت ہے کہ ہم پھر بھی جیئے جاتے ہیں

زندگی کیا کسی مُفلس کی قَبا ہے جس میں

ہر گھڑی درد کے پیوند لگے جاتے ہیں

لیکن اب ظلم کی میعاد کے دن تھوڑے ہیں

اک ذرا صبر، کہ فریاد کے دن تھوڑے ہیں

عرصۂ دہر کی جُھلسی ہوئی ویرانی میں

ہم کو رہنا ہے پہ یونہی تو نہیں رہنا ہے

اجنبی ہاتھوں کا بے نام گرانبار ستم

آج سہنا ہے، ہمیشہ تو نہیں سہنا ہے

یہ ترے حُسن سے لپٹی ہوئی آلام کی گرد

اپنی دوروزہ جوانی کی شکستوں کا شمار

چاندنی راتوں کا بے کار دہکتا ہوا درد

دل کی بے سُود تڑپ، جسم کی مایوس پکار

چند روز اور مری جان! فقط چند ہی روز

A Few Days More, My Love!

A few days more, my love! A few days!

Forced to breathe beneath the shadow of tyranny;

A while longer, let us tremble, let us weep:

A legacy of our ancestors, we are blameless for this.

Our bodies are shackled, our passions enchained,

Our thought jailed, and our speech censored;

Our strength is that we struggle on, living.

Is life some beggar's ragged coat

Patched every moment with pain?

But now, the days that mark the tyrant's rule are few;

A little patience, our days of lamentation are few.

In the scorched desert spanned by this age

We must live, but not like this.

The oppressive burden of nameless foreign hands

We must endure today, though not forever.

This torment smearing your beauty like dust,

Reckoning the defeats of our short-lived youth,

The burning useless pain of moonlit nights,

The heart's empty anguish, the body's hopeless cry—

A few days more, my love! A few days!

موضوعِ سخن

گُل ہوئی جاتی ہے افسردہ سُلگتی ہوئی شام

دُھل کے نکلے گی ابھی چشمۂ مہتاب سے رات

اور مشتاق نگاہوں کی سنی جائے گی

اور اُن ہاتھوں سے مَس ہوں گے یہ ترسے ہوئے ہاتھ

اِن کا آنچل ہے، کہ رُخسار، کہ پیراہن ہے

کچھ تو ہے جس سے ہوئی جاتی ہے چلمن رنگیں

جانے اس زلف کی موہوم گھنی چھاؤں میں

ٹمٹماتا ہے وہ آویزہ ابھی تک کہ نہیں

آج پھر حسنِ دل آرا کی وہی دھج ہوگی

وہی خوابیدہ سی آنکھیں، وہی کاجل کی لکیر

رنگِ رخسار پہ ہلکا سا وہ غازے کا غبار

صندلی ہاتھ پہ دُھندلی سی حِنا کی تحریر

اپنے افکار کی، اشعار کی دنیا ہے یہی

جانِ مضموں ہے یہی، شاہدِ معنٰی ہے یہی

آج تک سرخ و سیہ صدیوں کے سائے کے تلے

آدم و حوّا کی اولاد پہ کیا گزری ہے؟

موت اور زیست کی روزانہ صف آرائی میں

ہم پہ کیا گزرے گی، اجداد پہ کیا گزری ہے؟

اِن دمکتے ہوئے شہروں کی فراواں مخلوق

کیوں فقط مرنے کی حسرت میں جیا کرتی ہے؟

یہ حسیں کھیت، پھٹا پڑتا ہے جوبن جن کا!

The Theme of Poetry

Evening, spiritless, smoldering, is dying out;

Now Night, washed in fountained moonlight, will come,

And yearning eyes will have their fill,

These eager hands shall feel those.

Is it the edge of her veil, or cheek, or her dress

That tinges with color the curtain?

Who knows if in the deep fanciful shade of that tress

That earring still glimmers,

That same loveliness will grace this day:

Those same dreamy eyes, the same darkened lids

Faintly dusted with rouge, her cheek's color,

On her sandalwood-colored hand the misty inscription of henna.

This alone is the world of my thoughts, my verses,

This the essence of my composing, the witness of my meaning.

Until now, in the shadow of centuries, black and red,

What has overtaken the children of Eve and Adam?

In daily confrontation of death and life, arrayed for war,

What will befall us, what befell our ancestors?

Countless creatures in all these glittering cities:

Do they live merely longing for death?

Why do these beauteous fields whose bloom breaks forth

کس لئے ان میں فقط بھوک اُگا کرتی ہے

یہ ہر اِک سمت پُراسرار کڑی دیواریں

جل بجھے جن میں ہزاروں کی جوانی کے چراغ

یہ ہر اک گام پہ اُن خوابوں کی مقتل گاہیں

جن کے پرتو سے چراغاں ہیں ہزاروں کے دماغ

یہ بھی ہیں، ایسے کئی اور بھی مضموں ہوں گے

لیکن اس شوخ کے آہستہ سے کُھلتے ہوئے ہونٹ

ہائے اس جسم کے کم بخت دلآویز خطوط

آپ ہی کہئے کہیں ایسے بھی افسوں ہوں گے

اپنا موضوعِ سخن ان کے سوا اور نہیں

طبعِ شاعر کا وطن ان کے سوا اور نہیں

Yield hunger as their harvest?

Walls, on every side, bursting with secrets:

Numberless youthful lanterns burnt to ashes;

At every step, the execution grounds of those dreams

Who illumined numberless minds;

These are themes also; many there may be,

But the slowly opening mouth of that passion!

The wretched curves, alas, of that alluring form!

What else could possess such enchantment?

The theme of my verse is nothing but these;

The poet's homeland finds its nature in these.

اے دلِ بیتاب ٹھہر!

تیرگی ہے کہ اُمنڈتی ہی چلی آتی ہے

شب کی رگ رگ سے لہو پھوٹ رہا ہو جیسے

چَل رہی ہے کچھ اس انداز سے نبضِ ہستی

دونوں کا عالم کا نشہ ٹوٹ رہا ہو جیسے

رات کا گرم لہو اور بھی بہ جانے دو

یہی تاریکی تو ہے غازۂ رخسارِ سحر

صبح ہونے ہی کو ہے اے دلِ بیتاب ٹھہر

ابھی زنجیر چھنکتی ہے پسِ پردۂ ساز

مطلق الحکم ہے شیرازۂ اسباب ابھی

ساغرِ ناب میں آنسو بھی ڈھلک جاتے ہیں

لغزشِ پا میں ہے پابندیٔ آداب ابھی

اپنے دیوانوں کو دیوانہ تو بن لینے دو

اپنے میخانوں کو میخانہ تو بن لینے دو

جلد یہ سطوتِ اسباب بھی اٹھ جائے گی

یہ گرانباریِ آداب بھی اٹھ جائے گی

خواہ زنجیر چھنکتی ہی رہی، چھنکتی ہی رہے

FROM *Dast-e Saba*
(Hand of the Zephyr)

Wait, O Restless Heart!

The darkness swells, overflowing,

Like blood spurting from every vein of night

Life's pulse beats as if

The two worlds were rising from intoxication.

Let night's warm blood flow some more:

This very darkness is the rouge of dawn's cheek.

Morning is almost here—wait, O restless heart!

Even now clanks a chain behind the veil of music:

Supreme power still rules the order of things;

Into the cup of pure wine run tears also;

Custom still shackles the stumbling foot.

Let true madness fill our madmen,

Let wine fill our wineshops!

Soon this grandeur of dictatorship shall be thrown off,

The burden of custom thrown off,

Though the chain clank and clank.

◯

صبا کے ہاتھ میں نرمی ہے ان کے ہاتھوں کی
ٹھہر ٹھہر کے یہ ہوتا ہے آج دل کو گماں
وہ ہاتھ ڈھونڈ رہے ہیں بساطِ محفل میں
کہ دل کے داغ کہاں ہیں نشستِ درد کہاں

طوق و دار کا موسم

روش روش ہے وہی انتظار کا موسم
نہیں ہے کوئی بھی موسم، بہار کا موسم

گراں ہے دل پہ غمِ روزگار کا موسم
ہے آزمائشِ حسنِ نگار کا موسم

خوشا نظارۂ رخسارِ یار کی ساعت
خوشا قرارِ دلِ بےقرار کا موسم

حدیثِ بادہ و ساقی نہیں تو کس مصرف
خرامِ ابر سرِ کوہسار کا موسم

نصیب صحبتِ یاراں نہیں تو کیا کیجے
یہ رقصِ سایۂ سرو و چنار کا موسم

Fragment

In the hand of the zephyr is the softness of her hands;

This thought comes stumbling to my heart today:

Those hands are seeking among the gathered company

The scars of the heart, the situations of pain.

The Season of Fetters and Gallows

The same season of waiting haunts every road,

No season brings the season of Spring,

Heavy on the heart is the daily pain of survival;

Now is the time to try the lover's beauty.

Blessed is the moment when a friend's face appears,

Blessed the heart's repose in a season of turmoil.

Without the custom of wine and Saqi, to what purpose

The season of clouds drifting over the mountain peak?

If friendly society is beyond us, what good is there

In this season where the shadows dance of cypress and poplar?

یہ دل کے داغ تو دکھتے تھے یوں بھی پر کم کم
کچھ اب کے اور ہے ہجرانِ یار کا موسم

یہی جنوں کا، یہی طوق و دار کا موسم
یہی ہے جبر، یہی اختیار کا موسم

قفس ہے بس میں تمہارے، تمہارے بس میں نہیں
چمن میں آتشِ گل کے نکھار کا موسم

صبا کی مست خرامی ترِ کمند نہیں
اسیرِ دام نہیں ہے بہار کا موسم

بلا سے ہم نے نہ دیکھا تو اور دیکھیں گے
فروغِ گلشن و صوتِ ہزار کا موسم

زنداں کی ایک شام

شام کے پیچ و خم ستاروں سے
زینہ زینہ اتر رہی ہے رات
یوں صبا پاس سے گزرتی ہے
جیسے کہہ دی کسی نے پیار کی بات
صحنِ زنداں کے بےوطن اشجار
سرنگوں، محو ہیں بنانے میں
دامنِ آسماں پہ نقش و نگار
شانۂ بام پر دمکتا ہے!

Such were the achings, though small, of these scars in the heart.

Greater are today's pains when friends are apart.

This is the season of madness, of fetters and gallows,

The season of compulsion, of choice.

Under your control is the cage, but not the season

In the garden of the rose's ruby fire.

The frenzied rush of the dawn wind fears no gallows,

The season of Spring cannot be snared.

If I do not see it, others will see the season

Of the rose garden's glory, the nightingale's song.

A Prison Evening

Night descends the stairway

Of evening's winding, tortuous stars;

The dawn breeze breathes close by

As if hearing words of love.

In the prison courtyard, trees with no homeland

Are engrossed, heads drooping, creating

Art in images on the sky's hem.

On the roof's crest gleams

مہرباں چاندنی کا دستِ جمیل

خاک میں گھل گئی ہے آبِ نجوم

نور میں گھل گیا ہے عرش کا نیل

سبز گوشوں میں نیلگوں سائے

لہلہاتے ہیں جس طرح دل میں

موجِ دردِ فراقِ یار آئے

دل سے پیہم خیال کہتا ہے

اتنی شیریں ہے زندگی اس پل

ظلم کا زہر گھولنے والے

کامراں ہو سکیں گے آج نہ کل

جلوہ گاہِ وصال کی شمعیں

وہ بجھا بھی چکے اگر تو کیا؟

چاند کو گُل کریں تو ہم جانیں

Loving moonlight's lovely hand.

The stars' luster is melted in dust,

The azure of heaven is lost in light,

Deep-blue shadows in green corners

Ripple, as pain waves in the heart

For a distant lover.

My heart senses:

So sweet is life in this moment

That those who brew poisonous tyranny

Will succeed

Neither now nor tomorrow.

Let them, if they will, choke

Love's lanterns in the bridal chamber;

We shall worry when they snuff out

The very moon.

دریچہ

گڑی ہیں کتنی صلیبیں مرے دریچے میں

ہر ایک اپنے مسیحا کے خوں کا رنگ لئے

ہر ایک وصلِ خداوند کی امنگ لئے

کسی پہ کرتے ہیں ابرِ بہار کو قرباں

کسی پہ قتلِ مہِ تابناک کرتے ہیں

کسی پہ ہوتی ہے سر مست شاخسار دو نیم

کسی پہ بادِ صبا کو ہلاک کرتے ہیں

ہر آئے دن یہ خداوندگانِ مہر و جمال

لہو میں غرق مرے غمکدے میں آتے ہیں

اور آئے دن مری نظروں کے سامنے ان کے

شہید جسم سلامت اٹھائے جاتے ہیں

FROM *Zindan Namah*
(A Prison Narrative)

Window

How many crosses are buried in my window

Each stained with the blood of its own Messiah,

Each aspiring to unite with its god.

On one of them they sacrifice the Spring cloud,

On another they murder the moon's radiance,

On a third the bower of delight is rent in two,

On a fourth is slaughtered the morning breeze.

Each day, these godly beings of kindness and beauty

Come, dripping with blood, into my sorrowful cell,

And each day, before my eyes

The bodies of martyrs are raised up and healed.

آجاؤ، میں نے سُن لی ترے ڈھول کی ترنگ

آجاؤ، مست ہوگئی میرے لہو کی تال

"آجاؤ ایفریقا"[1]

آجاؤ، میں نے دھول سے ماتھا اُٹھا لیا

آجاو، میں نے چھیل دی آنکھوں سے غم کی چھال

آجاؤ، میں نے درد سے بازو چھڑا لیا

آجاو، میں نے نوچ دیا ہے کسی کا جال

"آجاؤ ایفریقا"

پنجے میں ہتھکڑی کی کڑی بن گئی ہے گرز

گردن کا طوق توڑ کے ڈھالی ہے میں نے ڈھال

"آجاؤ ایفریقا"

جلتے ہیں ہر کچھار میں بھالوں کے مرگ نین

دشمن لہو سے رات کی کالک ہوئی ہے لال

"آجاؤ ایفریقا"

دھرتی دھڑک رہی ہے مرے ساتھ ایفریقا

دریا تھرک رہا ہے تو بَن دے رہا ہے تال

میں ایفریقا ہوں، دھار لیا میں نے تیرا روپ

میں تو ہوں، میری چال ہے تیری ببر کی چال

"آجاؤ ایفریقا"

آؤ ببر کی چال

"آجاؤ ایفریقا"

---

[1] افریقی حریت پسندوں کا نعرہ

Come, Africa!

Come, I have heard the frenzy of your drums,

Come, the rhythm of my blood is wild,

Come, Africa![1]

Come, I have raised my forehead from the dust;

I have peeled the skin of grief from my eyes;

I have freed my arm from pain,

Come, Africa!

In my hand a link of the fetter becomes a mace,

I have molded a shield from the shattered chains around my neck,

Come, Africa!

On every riverbank burn spear points like gazelles' eyes;

Night's blackness is red with enemy blood:

Come, Africa!

The earth vibrates with me, Africa!

The river dances wildly while the jungle beats rhythm:

I am Africa, I have taken on your form,

I am you, my stride is your lion's stride,

Come, Africa!

Lion stride,

Come!

---

[1]Cry of the African freedom fighters

سفر نامہ

بساطِ رقص پہ صد شرق و غرب سے سر شام

دمک رہا ہے تری دوستی کا ماہِ تمام

چھلک رہی ہے ترے حُسنِ مہرباں کی شراب

بھرا ہوا ہے لبالب ہر اِک نگاہ کا جام

گلے میں تنگ ترے حرفِ لطف کی باہیں

پسِ خیال کہیں ساعتِ سفر کا پیام

ابھی سے یاد میں ڈھلنے لگی ہے صُحبتِ شب

ہر ایک روئے حسیں ہو چلا ہے بیش حسیں

ملے کچھ ایسے، جُدا یوں ہوئے کہ فیض اب کے

جو دل پہ نقش بنے گا وہ گُل ہے، داغ نہیں

FROM *Dast-e Tah-e Sang*
(Hand under the Stone)

Journey

On the dance floor, as east and west bring night,

Your friendship, like a full moon, burns with light;

Your loveliness is wine overflowing,

Your every glance a goblet, brimming bright.

Your gracious speech holds me in tight embrace;

Somewhere beneath thought, the dreaded hour of flight:

The evening's society melts into memory,

Each delightful face acquires more delight.

We met, O Faiz, and parted in such wise:

The heart is left marked with roses, not blight.

زندگی

شُکر کس طور سے ادا کیجے	ملکۂ شہرِ زندگی تیرا
تنگ دستی کا کیا گلہ کیجے	دولتِ دل کا کچھ شمار نہیں
ان کو تشویشِ روزگار کہاں؟	جو ترے حُسن کے فقیر ہوئے
اس سے خوش وقت کار و بار کہاں؟	درد بیچیں گے گیت گائیں گے
مِنّتِ لُطفِ غم گسار کسے؟	جام چھلکا تو جم گئی محفل
رنج کم ظرفیِ بہار کسے؟	اشک ٹپکا تو کھِل گیا گلشن
دَیر میں ہے نہ خانقاہ میں ہے	خوش نشیں ہیں کہ چشم و دل کی مراد
ہر صنم اپنی بارگاہ میں ہے	ہم کہاں قسمت آزمانے جائیں
نقدِ شمس و قمر کی بات کرے	کون ایسا غنی ہے جس سے کوئی
جائے تسخیرِ کائنات کرے	جس کو شوقِ نبرد ہو ہم سے

Existence

Queen of the city of existence,

How shall you know our gratitude?

There can be no account of the heart's wealth:

How can one groan of poverty?

Do those worshipers who beg your beauty

Struggle to live?

They shall sell sorrow, they shall sing songs:

What happier trade than this?

When the cup overflows, with the company assembled,

Who feels indebted to the consoler's grace?

When tears spill, the garden has bloomed:

Who is aggrieved at Spring's low spirit?

Blessed are we, that the longing of our eye and heart

Seeks neither temple nor monastery.

Where should we go to put fate to the test?

Our own mansion houses every idol.

Who owns wealth so vast as to bargain

A cash price for the sun and the moon?

Whoever, so eager, would do battle with us

Let him first subdue the universe.

قطعات

ڈھلتی ہے موجِ مَے کی طرح رات ان دِنوں
کھلتی ہے صبح گل کی طرح رنگ و بُو سے پُر
ویراں ہیں جام پاس کرو کچھ بہار کا
دل آرزو سے پُر کرو، آنکھیں لہُو سے پُر

پاس رہو

تم مرے پاس رہو
مرے قاتل، مرے دِلدار، مرے پاس رہو
جس گھڑی رات چلے،
آسمانوں کا لہو پی کے سیہ رات چلے
مرہمِ مُشک لئے، نشترِ الماس لئے
بَین کرتی ہوئی، ہنستی ہوئی، گاتی نکلے
درد کے کاسنی پازیب بجاتی نکلے
جس گھڑی سینوں میں ڈُوبے ہوئے دل
آستینوں میں نہاں ہاتھوں کی رہ تکنے لگیں
آس لئے
اور بچوں کے بلکنے کی طرح قلقلِ مَے
بہرِ ناسودگی مچلے تو مناۓ نہ منے
جب کوئی بات بناۓ نہ بنے
جب نہ کوئی بات چلے

Lines

Nowadays Night falls like flowing wine,

Dawn blooms like a rose, lush with fragrance and color;

Empty are the wine cups, pay heed to the Spring!

Fill the heart with desire, the eyes with blood!

Be near Me

Be near me,

My killer, my lover, be near me —

At the hour when Night strikes,

Black Night, gorged with heaven's blood,

Bearing musk scent and lancet of diamond,

When she comes, lamenting, laughing, singing,

Comes jingling blue anklets of pain,

At the hour when hearts, sunken in breasts,

Begin to watch for hands hidden in sleeves,

Bearing hope.

And gurgling wine, like the sobbing of children,

Discontent, is obstinate and will not be appeased.

When some goal eludes,

When no attempt succeeds,

جس گھڑی رات چلے

جس گھڑی ماتمی، سنسان، سیہ رات چلے

پاس رہو

مرے قاتل، مرے دلدار، مرے پاس رہو!

At the hour when Night, mournful,

Alone and black, comes,

Be near me,

My killer, my lover, be near.

N. M. RASHED

Nazar Muhammad Rashed (1910–75) was born in Akalgarh, west Pakistan. He produced four volumes of poetry between 1942 and 1975. He also published critical essays and later translated T. S. Eliot's essay "The Three Voices of Poetry." Rashed traveled widely, living for long periods in both Eastern and Western countries, an experiential synthesis reflected in his verse. He is one of the pioneers of modernist Urdu poetry, both in his subversion of traditional verse forms and in his expression of a secular outlook. His work integrates influences from Arab and Persian writers as well as from the French symbolists and Western modernist poets such as Eliot and Pound.

انتقام

اس کا چہرہ، اس کے خدّ و خال یاد آتے نہیں

اک شبستاں یاد ہے

اک برہنہ جسم آتشداں کے پاس

فرش پر قالین، قالینوں پہ سیج

دھات اور پتھر کے بت

گوشۂ دیوار میں ہنستے ہوئے!

اور آتشداں میں انگاروں کا شور

اُن بتوں کی بے حسی پر خشمگیں؛

اُجلی اُجلی اونچی دیواروں پہ عکس

اُن فرنگی حاکموں کی یادگار

جن کی تلواروں نے رکھا تھا یہاں

سنگِ بنیادِ فرنگ!

اُس کا چہرہ اس کی خدّ و خال یاد آتے نہیں

اک برہنہ جسم اب تک یاد ہے

اجنبی عورت کا جسم،

میرے "ہونٹوں" نے لیا تھا رات بھر

جس سے اربابِ وطن کی بے بسی کا انتقام

وہ برہنہ جسم اب تک یاد ہے!

FROM *Mawara* (**Beyond**)

Revenge

I don't remember her face or features;

I remember a room,

A naked body beside a fireplace,

A carpet on the floor, on the carpet a bed;

Images of bronze and stone

Laughing, in the wall's niche;

In the fireplace sparks crackling their fury

At the images, so inert,

And a reflection stains the white, white walls:

The souvenir of Western rulers

Whose swords placed here

The foundation stone of Europe.

I don't remember her face or features,

But I remember even now the naked body

Of a foreign woman, from which

My lips took all night

Revenge for the helpless owners of our homeland;

I remember.

خواب کی بستی

(سانیٹ)

مرے محبوب، جانے دے، مجھے اُس پار جانے دے

اکیلا جاؤں گا اور تیر کے مانند جاؤں گا

کبھی اِس ساحلِ ویران پر میں پھر نہ آؤں گا

گوارا کر خدا را اس قدر ایثار جانے دے!

نہ کر اب ساتھ جانے کے لئے اصرار جانے دے!

میں تنہا جاؤں گا، تنہا ہی تکلیفیں اُٹھاؤں گا

مگر اُس پار جاؤں گا تو شاید چین پاؤں گا

نہیں مجھ میں زیادہ ہمت تکرار جانے دے!

مجھے اُس خواب کی بستی سے کیا آواز آتی ہے؟

مجھے اس پار لینے کے لیے وہ کون آیا ہے؟

خدا جانے وہ اپنے ساتھ کیا پیغام لایا ہے

مجھے جانے دے اب رہنے سے میری جان جاتی ہے!

مرے محبوب، میرے دوست اب جانے بھی دے مجھ کو

بس اب جانے بھی دے اِس ارضِ بے آباد سے مجھ کو!

City of Dreams

Lover, there's the other shore! Let me go,

    I'll never return to this desolate

Place. You cannot come, let me greet my fate.

    Alone I will go and like an arrow:

For God's sake, have patience and let me go,

    Alone I'll suffer whatever hardships wait,

But there alone I'll find some path, some gate

    To peace. I've no strength to argue, let me go:

From the city of dreams what sounds beckon?

    Who comes to greet me on the other side?

What's his message, only God can reckon,

    Were I to stay, my soul would not abide;

Friend and lover, release me, let me go

    From these empty shores: you cannot follow.

Rashed uses a slight modification of the Petrarchan sonnet form, which I have attempted to reproduce here.

دریچے کے قریب

جاگ اے شمعِ شبستانِ وصال

مخمل خواب کے اس فرشِ طربناک سے جاگ !

لذتِ شب سے ترا جسم ابھی چور سہی -

آ مری جان، مرے پاس دریچے کے قریب

دیکھ کس پیار سے انوارِ سحر چومتے ہیں

مسجدِ شہر کے میناروں کو

جن کی رفعت سے مجھے

اپنی برسوں کی تمنا کا خیال آتا ہے !

سیمگوں ہاتھوں سے اے جاں ذرا

کھول مے رنگ جنوں خیز آنکھیں!

اسی مینار کو دیکھ

صبح کے نور سے شاداب سہی

اسی مینار کے سائے کے تلے کچھ یاد بھی ہے

اپنے بیکار خدا کے مانند

اُونگھتا ہے کسی تاریک نہاں خانے میں

ایک افلاس کا مارا ہوا ملّاءِ حزیں

ایک عفریت ---اُداس

تین سو سال کی ذلت کا نشان

ایسی ذلت کہ نہیں جس کا مداوا کوئی!

دیکھ بازار میں لوگوں کا ہجوم

بے پنا سیل کے مانند رواں!

Near the Window

Lamp of Love's chamber, awake!

Wake from this joyful floor of soft dreams,

Your body still tired from night's pleasure;

Come by me, lover, near the window

And see with what passion dawn's rays

Kiss the minarets of our city's mosque

Whose height brings to mind my

Age-long desire.

With your silver-white hands, my lover,

Open those wine-dark, bewildering eyes:

See this minaret

Watered by early light:

Beneath its shadow—do you remember?—

A mournful, penniless priest

Drowsing in some dark, hidden corner

Like his useless god:

A demon, dismayed!

Here is the stain of three hundred years,

An indignity without cure.

See the crowd in the marketplace

Moving, an endless flow.

جیسے جنّات بیابانوں میں
مشعلیں لے کے سرِشام نکل آئے ہیں،
ان میں ہر شخص کے سینے کے کسی گوشے میں
ایک دلہن سی بنی بیٹھی ہے
ٹمٹماتی ہوئی ننھی سی خودی کی قندیل
لیکن اتنی بھی توانائی نہیں
بڑھ کے ان میں سے کوئی شعلۂ جوّالہ بنے!
ان میں مفلس بھی ہیں، بیمار بھی ہیں
زیرِ افلاک مگر ظلم سہے جاتے ہیں!

ایک بوڑھا سا تھکا ماندہ سا رہوار ہوں میں!
بھوک کا شاہ سوار
سخت گیر اور تنومند بھی ہے؛
میں بھی اس شہر کے لوگوں کی طرح
ہر شبِ عیش گزر جانے پر
بہرِ جمعِ خس و خاشاک نکل جاتا ہوں
چرخ گرداں ہے جہاں
شام کو پھر اسی کاشانے میں لوٹ آتا ہوں
بے بسی میری ذرا دیکھ کہ میں
مسجدِ شہر کے میناروں کو
اس دریچے میں سے پھر جھانکتا ہوں
جب انہیں عالمِ رخصت میں شفق چومتی ہے!

As jinns[1] in the wastelands

Emerge at early evening, bearing torches,

A bridelike figure sits

In the corner of each man's heart:

The tiny lantern of Self flickers

Without strength to burst into

Spinning flame.

Among these are the poor, the sick

Enduring tyranny below the heavens.

I an old, weary, ambling horse

Ridden by Hunger, hard and robust,

I too, like others in the city

Go out, after each night of love, to

Gather all this rubbish

Where the sky is turning.

At night I return to this same house;

See my helplessness! I peer again

Through this window

At the minarets of our city's mosque

To see the red sky kiss them a sad farewell.

---

[1]Spirits, said in the Qur'an to be born of fire (50.14–15). They are often thought of as evil and as assuming fantastic forms.

سبا ویراں

سلیماں سر بزانو اور سبا ویراں
سبا ویراں، سبا آسیب کا مسکن
سبا آلام کا انبارِ بے پایاں!
گیاہ و سبزہ و گُل سے جہاں خالی
ہوائیں تَشنۂ باراں،
طَیور اس دشت کے مِنقار زیر پر
تو سُرمہ در گلو انساں
سلیماں سر بزانو اور سبا ویراں!

سلیماں سر بزانو، تُرشرو، غمگیں، پریشاں مُو
جہانگیری، جہانبانی، فقط طرّارۂ آہو،
محبت شعلۂ پرّاں، ہوس بُوئے گُلِ بے بُو
ز راز دہر کمتر گو!
سبا ویراں کہ اب تک اس زمیں پر ہیں
کسی عیّار کے غارتگروں کے نقشِ پا باقی
سبا باقی، نہ مہروئے سبا باقی!

FROM *Iran men Ajnabi*
(Foreigner in Iran)

Desolate Sheba

Solomon, head in his hands, and Sheba desolate,

Sheba desolate, the home of ghosts,

Sheba an endless heap of woes,

World devoid of grass, greenery, and flower,

Winds thirsty for rain,

Birds of the desert, beaks tucked beneath their wing

And men, choked on dust.

Solomon, head in his hands, bitterly disheveled hair,

World-dominion, world-administration, merely the bounding

of a deer;

Love a leaping flame, lust the odor of odorless flowers:

Speak less of the age's mysteries!

Sheba is wasted for on her soil

A cunning conqueror's ravaging prints are still seen

Sheba is no more, nor her beautiful queen.

Rashed's note on "Desolate Sheba" reads: "Solomon in this poem is a conqueror and lover who destroys what he conquers and kills what he loves, and in his old age is left with nothing except a deep remorse and a deep sense of futility. The poem has an allegorical reference to the politicians or dictators of today, who in their keenness to set things in order often end up doing exactly the opposite" ("Brief Note on My Poetry" [unpublished ms.]).

سلیماں سربزانو،

اب کہاں سے قاصدِ فرخندہ پَے آئے؟

کہاں سے، کس سبو سے کاسۂ پیری میں مے آئے؟

Solomon, head in his hands:

From where now will come a joyful envoy?

From where, which jar, will come wine into

The bowl of old age?

آئنہ حِسّ و خبر سے عاری!

آئنہ حِسّ و خبر سے عاری،
اُس کے نابود کو ہم ہست بنائیں کیسے؟
منحصر ہست تگاپوئے شب و روز پہ ہے
دلِ آئینہ کو آئینہ دکھائیں کیسے؟

دلِ آئینہ کی پہنائی بے کار پہ ہم روتے ہیں،
ایسی پہنائی کہ سبزہ ہے نمو سے محروم
گلِ نو رُستہ ہے بو سے محروم!
آدمی چشم و لب و گوش سے آراستہ ہیں
لطفِ ہنگامہ سے نورِ من و تو سے محروم!
مے چھلک سکتی نہیں، اشک کے مانند یہاں
اور نشّے کی تجلّی بھی جھلک سکتی نہیں
نہ صفائے دلِ آئینہ میں شورش کا جمال
نہ خلائے دلِ آئینہ گذرگاہِ خیال!

آئنہ حِسّ و خبر سے عاری
اس کے نابود کو ہم ہست بنائیں کیسے؟

FROM *La = Insan* (X = Man)

Mirror, Void of Sense and Knowledge

Mirror, void of sense and knowledge,

How should we turn its nothingness to being?

Being rests on the frenzied search of night and day.

How should we show a mirror's heart

A mirror?

We mourn that heart's futile expanse

Dry of foliage

Where the lately blossomed flower gives no smell.

Men, though beautified with eye, lip, and ear,

Are deprived

Of excitement, of the light

Of you and me.

Here wine cannot flow like tears

Nor intoxication glow

Nor lovely frenzy stir the mirror's pure heart.

Imagination finds no path through its emptiness.

Mirror, void of sense and knowledge,

How shall its nothingness assume being?

آئنہ ایسا سمندر ہے جسے
کردیا دستِ فسوں گر نے ازل میں ساکن!
عکس پر عکس در آتا ہے یہ امید لیے
اس کے دم ہی سے فسونِ دلِ تنہا ٹوٹے
یہ سکوتِ اجل آسا ٹوٹے !

آئینہ ایک پر اسرار جہاں میں اپنے
وقت کی اوس کے قطروں کی صدا سنتا ہے،
عکس کو دیکھتا ہے، اور زباں بند ہے وہ
شہر مدفون کے ماند ہے وہ!
اس کے نابود کو ہم ہست بنائیں کیسے؟
آئنہ حِسّ و خبر سے عاری !

اے غزالِ شب!

اے غزالِ شب،
تری پیاس کیسے بجھاؤں میں
کہ دکھاؤں میں وہ سراب جو مری جاں میں ہے؟
وہ سراب ساحرِ خوف ہے
جو سحر سے شام کے رہگذر
میں فریبِ رہرو سادہ ہے

The mirror is a sea, silenced

At Creation by a magic hand.

Image on image enters, hoping to

Break this lonely heart's charm, to

Shatter its deathlike calm.

In its dark world the mirror

Hears the drops of time's dew,

Watching reflections, its speech entombed

Like a buried city.

Gazelle of Night

O gazelle of night,

How shall I slake your thirst

Or show you the mirage in my soul?

That mirage, fearful sorcerer

Who beguiles the heedless traveler

On the road from dawn till night,

وہ سراب زادہ، سراب گر، کہ ہزار صورتِ نو بنو

میں قدم قدم پہ ستادہ ہے،

وہ جو غالب و ہمہ گیر دشتِ گماں میں ہے

مرے دل میں جیسے یقین بن کے سما گیا

مرے ہست و بود پہ چھا گیا!

اے غزالِ شب،

اُسی فتنہ کار سے چھپ گئے

مرے دیر و زود بھی خواب میں

مرے نزد و دور حجاب میں

وہ حجاب کیسے اٹھاؤں میں جو کشیدہ قالبِ دل میں ہے

کہ میں دیکھ پاؤں درونِ جاں

جہاں خوف و غم کا نشاں نہیں

جہاں یہ سراب رواں نہیں،

اے غزالِ شب!

Child of mirage, mirage maker

Hovering behind every step

In a thousand ever-changing faces,

This despot over uncertain deserts

Has possessed me like a belief.

My life filled with his darkness.

O gazelle of night, that miscreant lost

In dreams my befores and afters,

In veils my nears and fars,

How shall I lift the veil

Drawn across my heart's frame

To look inside my soul

Where fear and grief have no claim

And faded is this mirage,

O gazelle of night?

حسن کوزہ گر

جہاں زاد، نیچے گلی میں ترے در کے آگے

یہ میں سوختہ سر حسن کوزہ گر ہوں!

تجھے صبح بازار میں بوڑھے عطّار یوسف

کی دکّان پر میں نے دیکھا

تو تیری نگاہوں میں وہ تابناکی

تھی میں جس کی حسرت میں نو سال دیوانہ پھرتا رہا ہوں

جہاں زاد، نو سال دیوانہ پھرتا رہا ہوں!

یہ وہ دَور تھا جس میں میں نے

کبھی اپنے رنجور کوزوں کی جانب

پلٹ کر نہ دیکھا——

وہ کوزے مرے دستِ چابک کے پُتلے

گِل و رنگ و روغن کی مخلوقِ بے جاں

وہ سر گوشیوں میں یہ کہتے

"حسن کوزہ گر اب کہاں ہے؟

وہ ہم سے خود اپنے عمل سے

خداوند بن کر خداؤں کے مانند ہے روئے گرداں!"

جہاں زاد نو سال کا دور یوں مجھ پہ گزرا

کہ جیسے کسی شہر مدفون پر وقت گزرے؛

تغاروں میں مٹی

کبھی جس کی خوشبو سے وارفتہ ہوتا تھا میں

سنگ بستہ پڑی تھی

صراحی و مینا و جام و سبو اور فانوس و گلداں

Hassan the Potter

Jahan-zad,[1] below in the street, before your door

Here I stand, heart aflame, Hassan the potter!

This morning in the bazaar, at old man

Yousuf the perfumist's shop, I saw you

And in your eyes was that fire

In whose longing I have wandered mad for nine years.

Jahan-zad, for nine years I have wandered mad!

Lost in that desire,

I never turned toward my sad pots,

Those images of my restless hands,

Lifeless creations of dust and color and oil.

Now they whisper:

"Where is Hassan the potter?

Creating us, he's become a god!

And, like the gods, he turns away from us!"

Jahan-zad, nine years passed over me

As time treads over some buried city.

Dust in flowerpots

Whose aroma I'd fondly breathe

Was now overladen with stones.

Goblet, enamel, cup, pitcher, lantern, flower vase,

---

[1] A female name, sounding like many used in *The Arabian Nights*

مری ہیچ مایہ معیشت کے، اظہارِ فن کے سہارے

شکستہ پڑے تھے

میں خود، میں حسن کوزہ گر پا بہ گِل خاک بر سر برہنہ

سرِ "چاک" ژولیدہ مو، سر بزانو

کسی غمزدہ دیوتا کی طرح واہمہ کے

گِل و لا سے خوابوں کے سیّال کوزے بناتا رہا تھا۔

جہاں زاد، نو سال پہلے

تو ناداں تھی لیکن تجھے یہ خبر تھی

کہ میں نے، حسن کوزہ گر نے

تری قاف کی سی افق تاب آنکھوں

میں دیکھی ہے وہ تابناکی

کہ جس سے مرے جسم و جاں، ابر و مہتاب کا

رہگزر بن گئے تھے

جہاں زاد بغداد کی خواب گوں رات

وہ رودِ دجلہ کا ساحل

وہ کشتی وہ ملّاح کی بند آنکھیں

کسی خستہ جاں رنج بر کوزہ گر کے لیے

ایک ہی رات وہ کہربا تھی

کہ جس سے ابھی تک ہے پیوست اس کا وجود———

اس کی جاں اس کا پیکر

مگر ایک ہی رات کا ذوق دریا کی وہ لہر نکلا

حسن کوزہ گر جس میں ڈوبا تو اُبھرا نہیں ہے!

All hope of an art to express

My worthless existence

Lay dead,

And I, Hassan the potter, dust on my head,

Disheveled hair, prostrate on the potter's wheel

Like some downcast god

Creating pots in a dream world of being and nothing,

Saw, in your bright eyes of Caucasus

That fire

Through which my body and soul became wayfarers

Of cloud and moonlight.

Jahan-zad, that dreamy night in Baghdad,

The bank of the river Tigris,

The ship, the closed eyes of that sailor

For some weary, disheartened potter

One night alone was alive,

Which even now claims his

Spirit, his body,

Only one night's joy the river's wave has granted

In which Hassan the potter sunk, never to emerge

جہاں زاد اس دور میں روز، ہر روز

وہ سوختہ بخت آکر

مجھے دیکھتی چاک پر پا بہ گِل سر بزانو

تو شانوں سے مجھ کو ہلاتی——

(وہی چاک جو سالہا سال جینے کا تنہا سہارا تھا!)

وہ شانوں سے مُجھ کو ہلاتی

"حسن کوزہ گر ہوش میں آ

حسن اپنے ویران گھر پر نظر کر

یہ بچّوں کے تنّور کیونکر بھریں گے

حسن، اے محبت کے مارے

محبت امیروں کی بازی،

حسن، اپنے دیوار و در پر نظر کر"

مرے کان میں یہ نوائے حزیں یوں تھی جیسے

کسی ڈوبتے شخص کو زیرِ گرداب کوئی پکارے!

وہ اشکوں کے انبار پُھولوں کے انبار تھے ہاں

مگر مَیں حَسن کوزہ گر شہرِ اوہام کے اُن

خرابوں کا مجذوب تھا جن

میں کوئی صدا کوئی جنبش

کِسی مرغِ پرّاں کا سایہ

کِسی زندگی کا نشاں تک نہیں تھا!

And now, Jahan-zad, each day

That unlucky one comes to haunt me

Prostrated on the potter's wheel,

It shakes me by the shoulders

(The wheel that year to year was my only hope of livelihood).

"Hassan the potter, come to your senses,

Cast an eye on your ruined home.

How shall the bellies of these children be filled?

Hassan, Love's fool!

Leave that sport of the rich

And look to your own house."

In my ear that sorry voice fell

Like one calling down a whirlpool to a drowning man.

Yes, that lake of tears fed life to flowers,

But I, Hassan the potter, was enchanted

By ruins of the city of illusions

With no sound, no motion,

No shadow of a bird in flight,

No trace of life.

جہان زاد، میں آج تیری گلی میں

یہاں رات کی سردگوں تیرگی میں

ترے در کے آگے کھڑا ہوں

سر و مو پریشاں

دریچے سے وہ قاف کی سی طلسمی نگاہیں

مجھے آج پھر جھانکتی ہیں

زمانہ، جہاں زاد وہ چاک ہے جس پہ مینا و جام و سبو

اور فانوس و گُلداں

کے مانند بنتے بگڑتے ہیں انساں

مَیں انساں ہوں لیکن

یہ نو سال جو غم کے قالب میں گُزرے!

حسن کوزہ گر آج اک تودۂ خاک ہے جس

میں نم کا اثر تک نہیں ہے

جہاں زاد بازار میں صبح عطّار یوسف

کی دُکّان پر تیری آنکھیں

پھر اک بار کُچھ کہہ گئی ہیں

ان آنکھوں کی تابندہ شوخی

سے اُٹھی ہے پھر تودۂ خاک میں نم کی ہلکی سی لرزش

یہی شاید اس خاک کو گِل بنا دے

تمنّا کی وسعت کی کس کو خبر ہے جہاں زاد لیکن

تُو چاہے تو بن جاؤں مَیں پھر

وہی کوزہ گر جس کے کوزے

Jahan-zad, in your street today

Against night's chilling darkness

I stand restless before your door.

Through the window, those enchanting eyes

Peer at me again.

The age, Jahan-zad, is a potter's wheel on which

Like enamel, cup, pitcher,

Lantern, and flower vase

Humans are created and destroyed.

I am human, yet

These nine years have passed in the shape of grief.

Hassan the potter is today a heap of dust

Without sign of moisture.

Jahan-zad, this morning in the bazaar at

Yousuf the perfumist's shop, your eyes

Have spoken once again,

Breathing moisture into dust.

Perhaps dust will waken into clay.

Who knows the expanse of desire, Jahan-zad, but

If you wish, I'll become once more

That same potter whose pots

تھے ہر کاخ و کُو اور ہر شہر و قریہ کی نازش

تھے جن سے امیر و گدا کے مساکن درخشاں

تمنّا کی وسعت کی کس کو خبر ہے جہاں زاد لیکن

تُو چاہے تو میں پھر پلٹ جاؤں اُن اپنے ہجور کوزوں کی جانب

گِل و لا کے سوکھے تغاروں کی جانب

معیشت کے، اظہار فن کے سہاروں کی جانب

کہ مَیں اُس گِل و لا سے، اُس رنگ و روغن

سے پھر وہ شرارے نکالوں کہ جن سے

دِلوں کے خرابے ہوں روشن!

Were the pride of every palace and quarter, every city and village,

Adorning the dwellings of rich and poor.

Who knows the expanse of desire, Jahan-zad, but

If you wish, I'll turn once more toward my sad pots

Those dried pans of being and nothing,

Toward hope of an art to mirror my livelihood,

From that being and nothing, from that color and oil

To strike again the sparks by which

The ruins of hearts are illumined.

زندگی اک پیرہ زن

‫ـــــ زندگی اک پیرہ زن!‬
‫جمع کرتی ہے گلی کوچوں میں روز و شب پرانی دھجّیاں!‬
‫تیز، غم انگیز، دیوانہ ہنسی سے خندہ زن‬
‫بال بکھرے، دانت میلے، پیرہن‬
‫دھجّیوں کا ایک سونا اور ناپیدا کراں، تاریک بن!‬

‫ـــــ لو ہوا کے ایک جھونکے سے اُڑی ہیں ناگہاں‬
‫ہاتھ سے اس کے پرانے کاغذوں کی بالیاں‬
‫اور وہ آپے سے باہر ہو گئی‬
‫اس کی حالت اور ابتر ہو گئی‬
‫سہہ سکے گا کون یہ گہرا زیاں؟‬

‫ـــــ اب ہوا سے ہار تھک کر جھک گئی ہے پیرہ زن‬
‫جھک گئی ہے پاؤں پر، جیسے دفینہ ہو وہاں!‬
‫زندگی، تو اپنے ماضی کے کنوئیں میں جھانک کر کیا پائے گی؟‬
‫اس پرانے اور زہریلی ہواؤں سے بھرے، سونے کنوئیں میں‬
‫جھانک کر اس کی خبر کیا لائے گی؟‬
‫ـــــ اس کی تہہ میں سنگریزوں کے سوا کچھ بھی نہیں‬
‫جز صدا کچھ بھی نہیں!‬

Life an Old Hag

Life, an old hag

Gathering rags

Night and day in street and alley;

Cunning, pitiful, with a mad laugh,

Unkempt hair, and dirty teeth,

Her clothes an empty dark

Forest of rags.

See, the wind blasts from her hand

Old paper earrings,

And she

Turns over in fury!

More wretched than before:

Who could bear such deep loss?

Vanquished by the wind, she bends, fatigued

As if finding treasure at her feet;

Life, what will you find, peering

Into the well of your past?

What news will you bring

From an empty well's putrid, poisonous air?

At its bottom, nothing but pebbles,

Nothing but an echo.

آرزو راہبہ ہے

—— آرزو راہبہ ہے بے کس و تنہا و حزیں
آرزو راہبہ ہے، عمر گزاری جس نے
انہی محرومِ ازل راہبوں، معبد کے نگہبانوں میں
ان مہر و سالِ یک آہنگ کے ایوانوں میں!
کیسے معبد پہ ہے تاریکی کا سایہ بھاری
روئے معبود سے ہیں خون کے دھارے جاری

—— راہبہ رات کو معبد سے نکل آتی ہے
جھلملاتی ہوئی اک شمع لیے
لڑکھڑاتی ہوئی، فرش و در و دیوار سے ٹکراتی ہوئی!
دل میں کہتی ہے کہ اس شمع کی لَو ہی شاید
دُور معبد سے بہت دور چمکتے ہوئے انوار کی تمثیل بنے
آنے والی سحرِ نو یہی قندیل بنے!

—— آرزو راہبہ ہے بے کس و تنہا و حزین
ہاں مگر راہبوں کو اس کی خبر ہو کیونکر
خود میں کھوئے ہوئے، سہمے ہوئے، سرگوشی سے ڈرتے ہوئے
راہبوں کو یہ خبر ہو کیونکر
کس لیے راہبہ ہے بے کس و تنہا و حزیں!
راہب استادہ ہیں مرمر کے سلوں کے ماند

Desire Is a Nun

Desire is a nun, forlorn, lonesome, sad,

Passing her days among

These eternally deprived monks, guardians of the temple,

In these palaces of unmoving months and years.

On the temple falls a huge shadow,

Blood streaking from the face of the worshiped.

The nun fumbles out of the temple at night,

In her hand a flickering lamp,

Staggering, stumbling against walls and doors;

In her heart she says, perhaps this lamp's flame

Will be like the brilliance shining far from the temple,

The torch of approaching dawn.

Desire is a nun, forlorn and sad,

But how should monks know this:

Lost in themselves, terrified even of whispers,

How could monks know

Why the nun is sad?

Standing as they do, like marble slabs

In Islam there are no nuns; Rashed is probably speaking about a Christian nun in an Indian convent.

بے کراں عجز کی جاں سوختہ ویرانی میں
جس میں اُگتے نہیں دل سوزیٔ انساں کے گلاب!

راہبہ شمع لیے پھرتی ہے
یہ سمجھتی ہے کہ اس سے در معبد پہ کبھی
گھاس پر اوس جھلک اٹھے گی
سنگریزوں پہ کوئی چاپ سنائی دے گی!

In the soul-burning wilderness of

Endless submission

Where man's passion

Is a wilting rose.

The nun wanders, lamp in hand.

Stood at the temple door, she thinks its light

Might make the grass glimmer with dew

And over pebbles she might hear

A footstep.

وہ حرفِ تنہا
(جسے تمنائے وصلِ معنا)

ہمارے اَعضا جو آسماں کی طرف دعا کے لیے اٹھے ہیں،
(تم آسماں کی طرف نہ دیکھو!)
مقامِ نازک پہ ضربِ کاری سے جاں بچانے کا ہے وسیلہ
کہ اپنی محرومیوں سے چُھپنے کا یک حیلہ؟
بزرگ و برتر خدا کبھی تو (بہشت بر حق،)
ہمیں خدا سے نجات دے گا
کہ ہم ہیں اس سرزمیں پہ جیسے وہ حرفِ تنہا،
(مگر وہ ایسا جہاں نہ ہوگا) خموش و گویا،
جو آرزوئے وصالِ معنی میں جی رہا ہو
جو حرف و معنی کی یک دلی کو ترس گیا ہو!

ہمیں معرّی کے خواب دے دو
(کہ سب کو بخشیں بقدرِ ذوقِ نگہ تبسم)
ہمیں معرّی کی روح کا اِضطراب دے دو
(جہاں گناہوں کے حوصلے سے ملے تقدّس کے دکھ کا مرہم)
کہ اُس کی بے نور و تار آنکھیں
درونِ آدم کی تیرہ راتوں
کو چھیدتی تھیں

That Lonesome Word
(That Desires to Unite with Meaning)

Our limbs, raised in prayer toward the sky:

(Don't look at the sky!)

Is this to bypass harm in a fragile place

Or a pretext for hiding from our deprivations?

That ancient and high god (Paradise in truth)

Shall one day deliver us from god,

For we are on this earth as a lonesome Word[1]

(But it won't be a world like this) silent and speaking

That lives in desire for accord with meaning.

Grant us the dream of M'arri[2]

(Grant each a smile fitting his vision's breadth),

Grant us the vexation of M'arri's soul

(Where our bold sins will cure all pious misery),

For his dark, unlit eyes

Would pierce

The dark nights of Man's soul.

---

[1] Deliberately capitalized to imply Logos
[2] An eleventh-century Arab thinker, orphaned and blinded as a child, who was skeptical of God's existence

اُسی جہاں میں فراقِ جاں کاہِ حرف و معنٰی

کو دیکھتی تھیں

بہشت اُس کے لیے وہ معصوم سادہ لَوحوں کی عافیت تھا

جہاں وہ ننگے بدن پہ جابر کے تازیانوں سے بچ کے

راہِ فرار پائیں

وہ کفشِ پا تھا، کہ جس سے غُربت کی ریگِ بریاں

سے روز فُرصت قرار پائیں

کہ صُلبِ آدم کی، رحمِ حوّا کی عُزلتوں میں

نہایتِ انتظار پائیں!

(بہشت صِفَرِ عظیم، لیکن ہمیں وہ گم گَشتہ ہندسے ہیں

بغیر جن کے کوئی مساوات کیا بنے گی

وصالِ معنٰی سے حرف کی بات کیا بنے گی؟)

ہم اس زمیں پر ازل سے پیرانہ سر ہیں، مانا

مگر ابھی تک ہیں دل توانا

اور اپنی ژولیدہ کاریوں کے طُفیل دانا

ہمیں معّری کے خواب دے دو

(بہشت میں بھی نشاط، یک رنگ ہو تو، غم ہے

ہو ایک سا جامِ شہد سب کے لیے تو سَم ہے)

کہ ہم ابھی تک ہیں اس جہاں میں وہ حرفِ تنہا

(بہشت رکھ لو، ہمیں خود اپنا جواب دے دو!)

جسے تمنّائے وصلِ معنا . . . .

In that world they would see

The chasm between meanings and soul-consuming words.

Paradise, for him, was the bliss of simpletons,

A refuge from tyrants' whips.

The Word was the footprint that might lead them

From the burning sand of estrangement,

And in the loneliness of Adam's offspring

In Eve's womb, they might find an

End to their waiting.

(Paradise a vast zero; we are the missing term;

Without us what equation can hold?

What talk of union between word and meaning?)

Since time began we

Are on this earth as old men,

But the heart is still strong

And wise through folly.

Grant us the dream of M'arri.

(If in Paradise there's joy—and logic—there's grief also.

If there's honey, there's poison too.)

For we are still in this world a lonesome Word

(Keep your Paradise, show us our equal!)

That longs to kiss the lips of meaning.

MIRAJI

Miraji (1912–49), whose real name was Muhammad Sana'ullah, was born in West Punjab, Pakistan. He dropped out of high school and wrote for various literary journals, notably the political journal *Adabi Dunya*, in Lahore, for which he was deputy editor between 1938 and 1941. He then worked for three years at All India Radio in Delhi and wrote for journals such as *Saqi*. Moving to Bombay, he edited the journal *Khayal* from 1945 to 1949. He died in King Edward Hospital, Bombay. He spent his last days with his friend Akhtar ul-Iman, who poignantly portrayed the tragic end of this remarkable man: alienated, an alcoholic, and unwilling to be cured of his complexes. Miraji's poetry, highly allusive and symbolic, shows the influence of Indian writers as well as of the French symbolists; it gives expression, sometimes controversially, to sensual themes, unconscious desires and motives.

دُور و نزدیک

ترا دل دھڑکتا رہے گا

مِرا دل دھڑکتا رہے گا

مگر دُور دُور!

زمیں پر سہانے سمے آکے جاتے رہیں گے

یونہی دور دور!

ستارے چمکتے رہیں گے

یونہی دور دور!

ہر اک شے رہے گی

یونہی دُور دُور!

مگر تیری چاہت کا جذبہ،

یہ وحشی سا نغمہ،

رہے گا ہمیشہ

مِرے دل کے اندر

مِرے پاس پاس۔

FROM *Kulliyat-e Miraji*
(Collected Works)

Far and Near

Your heart will go on pounding.

My heart will pound

Though far, far away.

This soil shall see joyous times come and go,

Far, far away.

Stars will go on shimmering,

Also far.

Every object will remain

Far,

But this passion, this desire for you,

This wild song

Will stay inside my heart

Forever

Near.

لبِ جوئبارے

ایک ہی پل کے لئے بیٹھ کے پھر اٹھ بیٹھی
آنکھ نے صرف یہ دیکھا کہ نشستہ بت ہے،
یہ بصارت کو نہ تھی تاب کہ وہ دیکھ سکے
کیسے تلوار چلی، کیسے زمیں کا سینہ
ایک لمحے کے لئے چشمے کی مانند بنا۔

پیچ کھاتے ہوئے یہ لہر اٹھی دل میں مرے
کاش! یہ جھاڑیاں اک سلسلۂ کوہ بنیں۔
دامنِ کوہ میں مَیں جا کے ستادہ ہوجاؤں۔
ایسی انہونی جو ہوجائے تو کیوں یہ نہ ہو
خشک پتّوں کا زمیں پر جو بجھا ہے بستر
وہ بھی اک ساز بنے ۔۔۔۔ ساز تو ہے، ساز تو ہے
نغمہ بیدار ہوا تھا جو ابھی، کان تِرے
کیوں اُسے سن نہ سکے سننے سے مجبور رہے
پردۂ چشم نے صرف ایک نشستہ بُت کو
ذہن کے دائرۂ خاص میں مرکوز کیا۔

یاد آتا ہے مجھے ۔۔۔۔ کان ہوئے تھے بیدار
خشک پتّوں سے جب آئی تھی تڑپنے کی صدا،
اور دامن کی ہر اک لہر چمک اٹھی تھی،
پڑ رہا تھا اسی تلوار کا سایہ شاید
جو نکل آئی تھی اک پل میں نہاں خانے سے

Bank of the River

For one moment only, my eye saw it,

A seated idol;

My vision lacked strength to see

How the sword flashed, how the earth's breast

Rose, for an instant, like a fountain.

In my heart arose a rippling wave:

If these trees were a mountain range

At whose foot I might stand;

And the dry leaf bed, strewn upon the ground,

Rise into music—music it is.

The song awoke which, till now, was beyond

Hearing.

The eye's veil has placed a seated idol

Within the mind's private horizon.

I remember—my ears awoke

To the sound of rustling from dry leaves,

Each contour glimmering of the mountain's foot,

Perhaps the shadow falling of that very sword

Flashing abruptly from a concealed draw

جیسے بے ساختہ انداز میں بجلی چمکے

لیکن اس دامنِ آلودہ کی ہر لہر مٹی-
جل پری دیکھتے ہی دیکھتے روپوش ہوئی،
میں ستادہ ہی رہا، میں نے نہ دیکھا (افسوس!)
کیسے تلوار چلی، کیسے زمیں کا سینہ
ایک لمحے کےلئے چشمے کی مانند بنا-

دامنِ کوہ میں استادہ نہیں ہوں اس وقت
جھاڑیاں سلسلۂ کوہ نہیں، پردہ ہیں
جس کے اس پار جھلکتا نظر آتا ہے مجھے
منظر انجان، اچھوتی سی دلہن کی صورت

ہاں، تصّور کو میں اب اپنے بنا کر دولہا
اسی پردے کے نہاں خانے میں لے جاؤں گا،
کیسے تلوار چلی، کیسے زمیں کا سینہ
دلِ بےتاب کی مانند تڑپ اٹھا تھا
ایک بےساختہ انداز میں، بجلی کی طرح
جل پری گوشۂ خلوت سے نکل آئی تھی!
زندگی گرم تھی ہر بوند میں آبی پاؤں
خشک پتّوں پہ پھسلتے ہوئے جا پہنچے تھے؛
میں بھی موجود تھا ——اک کرمکِ بے نام و نشاں

Like lightning, spontaneous.

Yet every wave vanished of this soiled mountain foot—

I spy the mermaid, she hides,

I remained standing: I did not see her, alas!

How the sword flashed, how the earth's breast

Rose, for an instant, like a fountain.

At the mountain's foot I no longer stand;

The trees are no mountain range, just a veil

On the other side of which I see glistening

A scene of mystery, a bride's innocent face.

I make my imagination a bridegroom.

I will lead him into this veil's hidden chamber.

How the sword flashed, how the earth's breast

Rose up like a restless heart

Flashing, lightning.

The mermaid emerged from her private corner!

Life was warm, in every raindrop a wet foot

Slithering on dry leaves;

I too was there—a firefly, anonymous,

میں نے دیکھا کہ گھٹا شق ہوئی، دھارا نکلی،
برق رفتاری سے اک تیر کماں نے چھوڑا،
اور وہ خم کھا کے، لچکتا ہوا تھرّا کے گِرا
قلّہِ کوہ سے گرتے ہوئے پتھّر کی طرح
کوئی بھی روک نہ تھی اس کے لئے، اس کے لئے
خشک پتّوں کا زمیں پر ہی بچھا تھا بستر،
اسی بستر پہ وہ انجان پری لیٹ گئی!

اور میں، کرمکِ بےنام، گھٹا کی صورت
اسی امّید میں تکتا رہا، تکتا ہی رہا
اب اسی وقت کوئی جل کی پری آ جائے۔
بنسری ہاتھ میں لے کر میں گوالا بن جاؤں،
جل پری آئے کہاں سے؟ وہ اسی بستر پر
میں نے دیکھا، ابھی آسودہ ہوئی، لیٹ گئی،
لیکن افسوس کہ میں اب بھی کھڑا ہوں تنہا،
ہاتھ آلودہ ہے، نمدار ہے، دھندلی نظر،
ہاتھ سے آنکھوں کے آنسو تو نہیں پونچھے تھے!

I saw the clouds split up, the rainy downpour

Shot, like lightning, from a bow,

Twisting, bending, it quivered and fell,

Falling from the mountain like a stone,

Nothing to stop it.

The dry leaf bed was strewn across the ground.

Here that mermaid, mysterious, lay.

And I, a nameless firefly, staring

At the heaps of cloud, hoping

The mermaid might now come,

And I, flute in hand, a cowherd.

I saw her, lying

Content, on this bed,

But alas I stand alone, still:

Hands smeared and wet, eyes misty.

No finger wiped the tears.

رس کی انوکھی لہریں

میں یہ چاہتی ہوں کہ دنیا کی آنکھیں مجھے دیکھتی جائیں، یوں دیکھتی جائیں جیسے

کوئی پیڑ کی نرم ٹہنی کو دیکھے،

(لچکتی ہوئی، نرم ٹہنی کو دیکھے)

مگر بوجھ پتّوں کا اترے ہوئے پیرہن کی طرح سیج کے
ساتھ ہی فرش پر ایک مسلا ہوا

ڈھیر بن کر پڑا ہو،

میں یہ چاہتی ہوں کہ جھونکے ہوا کے لپٹتے چلے جائیں مجھ سے،

مچلتے ہوئے، چھیڑ کرتے ہوئے، ہنستے ہنستے کوئی بات کہتے ہوئے، لاج کے بوجھ

سے رُکتے رُکتے، سنبھلتے ہوئے رس کی رنگین سرگوشیوں میں،

میں یہ چاہتی ہوں کبھی چلتے چلتے کبھی دوڑتے دوڑتے بڑھتی جاؤں۔

ہوا جیسے ندی کی لہروں سے چھوٹے ہوئے، سرسراتے ہوئے بہتی جاتی ہے، رُکتی

نہیں ہے،

اگر کوئی پنچھی سہانی صدا میں کہیں گیت گائے

تو آواز کی گرم لہریں مرے جسم سے آکے ٹکرائیں اور لوٹ جائیں، ٹھہرنے نہ پائیں،

کبھی گرم کرنیں، کبھی نرم جھونکے،

کبھی میٹھی میٹھی فسوں ساز باتیں،

کبھی کچھ کبھی کچھ نئے سے نیا رنگ اُبھرے،

اُبھرتے ہی تحلیل ہو جائے پھیلی فضا میں،

کوئی چیز میرے مسّرت کے گھیرے میں رکنے نہ پائے،

Strange Waves of Pleasure

I want the world's eyes to watch me, as if

> watching a tree's tender branch

(A tree's tender bowing branch),

The leafy burden heaped, like cast-off clothes, on the floor

> beside the bed.

I want the gusts of wind to go on embracing me,

Peevish, teasing, laughingly talking,

Hesitant with the burden of shame, needing support,

> in the colorful whispers of pleasure.

I wish to go on, walking, running,

Just as the wind caresses the rippling stream, rustling,

> flowing, unceasing.

If a bird should sing in charming notes,

Let the warm waves of sound sing against my body

> and return, without pause.

Warm rays, gentle breezes,

Sweet, enthralling words:

New things, new colors, always surfacing,

Surfacing and dissolving in the wide expanse.

Let nothing stay within the horizon of my rapture.

مسّرت کا گھیرا سمٹتا چلا جا رہا ہے

کُھلا کھیت گندم کا پھیلا ہوا ہے

بہت دور آکاش کا شامیانہ انوکھی مسہری رسیلے اشاروں سے بہکا

رہا ہے،

تھپیڑوں سے پانی کی آواز پنچھی کے گیتوں میں گُھل
کر پھسلتے ہوئے اب نگاہوں سے

اوجھل ہوئی جارہی ہے -

میں بیٹھی ہوئی ہوں

دوپٹہ میرے سر سے ڈھلکا ہوا ہے

مجھے دھیان آتا نہیں ہے : مِرے گیسوؤں کو کوئی دیکھ لے گا،

مسّرت کا گھیرا سمٹتا چلا جا رہا ہے،

بس اب اور کوئی نئی چیز میرے مسّرت کے گھیرے میں آنے نہ پائے

The horizon shrinks.

The field of wheat opens out;

The far sky's pavilion, an exotic bed,

Tempts with luscious gestures;

With a dashing of waves, the sound of water melts

      in birdsong, slipping

Hidden from eyes.

I am sitting,

My scarf slipped from my head.

Let them see my hair!

The horizon of pleasures narrows:

Let nothing new fall within my horizon of rapture.

ارتقاء

قدم قدم پر جنازے رکھے ہوئے ہیں ان کو اٹھاؤ، جاؤ!

یہ دیکھتے کیا ہو؟ کام میرا نہیں، تمہارا یہ کام ہے آج اور کل کا۔

تم آج میں محو ہوکے شاید یہ سوچتے ہو

نہ بیتا کل اور نہ آنے والا تمہارا کل ہے

مگر یونہی سوچ میں جو ڈوبے تو کچھ نہ ہوگا

جنازے رکھے ہوئے ہیں ان کو اٹھاؤ، جاؤ!

چلو! جنازوں کو اب اٹھاؤ۔

یہ بہتے آنسو بہیں گے کب تک؟ اٹھو اور اِن کو پونچھ ڈالو۔

یہ راستہ کب ہے؟ اک لحد ہے،

لحد کے اندر تو اک جنازہ ہی بار پائے گا یہ بھی سوچو۔

تو کیا مشیت کے فیصلے سے ہٹے ہٹے رینگتے رہوگے؟

جنازے رکھّے ہوئے ہیں ان کو اٹھاؤ، جاؤ۔

لحد ہے ایسے کہ جیسے بُھوکے کا لالچی منہ کھلا ہوا ہو

مگر کوئی تازہ ───── اور تازہ نہ ہو میسّر تو باسی لقمہ بھی اس کے اندر نہ جانے پائے

کھلا دہن یوں کھلا رہے جیسے اک خلا ہو

اٹھاؤ، جلدی اٹھاؤ، آنکھوں کے سامنے کچھ جنازے رکھّے ہوئے ہیں، ان کو اٹھاؤ، جاؤ،

لحد میں ان کو ابد کی اک گہری نیند میں غرق کرکے آؤ،

Evolution

At each step lie coffins; lift them and go!

What are you gazing at? This is not my work but yours,

    now and tomorrow—

Absorbed in the present, you may think

Your tomorrow is future and far,

But drowning like this in thought will do nothing:

The coffins are laid out, lift them and go!

Lift them now—

Until when will these tears run down? Rise and wipe them now—

This is no road, it is a grave

That can house but one coffin's load—

Will you crawl and crawl away from fate?

Here lie the coffins; take them and go—

The grave lies open: a hungry, greedy mouth:

Let it eat fresh morsels only, nothing stale!

The mouth opens like an empty space.

Quickly lift the coffins before you,

Lift them and go!

Sink them into the grave,

Into eternity's deep dream, then come back.

اگر یہ مُردے لحد کے اندر گئے تو شاید

تمہاری مردہ حیات بھی آج جاگ اٹھے

انجام

مجھے گِریہ سنائی دے رہا ہے

بہت ہی دور سے آتی ہوئی آواز ہے جیسے

کبھی لہروں میں گھل جائے، کبھی آگے نکل آئے،

یہ اس سونے سمے میں کس نے گہرا کر دیا دل کی اُداسی کو؟

نہیں، یہ عکس کب ہے، دور کی اک بات ہے

یہ گِریہ تو نہیں ہے، ایک لمحہ ہے

کہ جیسے صبح کا سورج شفق میں جاکے کھو جائے

اگر سورج شفق میں جاکے کھو جائے تو کیا پھر رات بھی

من موہنی ہوگی؟

ستارے تو مگر جن دور یوں سے جِھلملاتے ہیں

اُداسی کو بڑھاتے ہیں۔

شبِ تاریک تو بس جگمگاتے چاند ہی سے کچھ نکھرتی ہے

کہاں ہے چاند؟ اندھیری رات ہے، مجھے کو

اندھیری رات میں گِریہ سنائی دے رہا ہے

Let these corpses enter the grave,

Then your dead life might live.

Conclusion

I hear weeping,

Far away,

Now melting in waves, now breaking out in clear tones,

Who, in this void of time, has deepened the soul's sadness?

This is no reflection, merely a distant concern.

And this is not weeping, it is a moment

When the morning sun is lost in twilight:

If twilight drowns the sun, will night allure?

Yet the vast spaces across which stars glimmer

Deepen sadness—

The dark night is washed only by the gleaming moon.

The moon? It is deep night,

In which I hear deep lamentation

Or just a common sound, a moment lost

یہ گریہ تو نہیں ہے، ایک معمولی صدا ہے، وقت کے آغوش
میں کھویا ہوا لمحہ۔

زمانہ ایک بے پاں سمندر ہے
اور اس میں کس قدر بے کار آنسو ہیں
اور اس میں ساحلِ افسردہ کی کچھ سسکیاں ہیں
میں سب کچھ دیکھتا ہوں اور پھر ہنستا ہوں، روتا ہوں
یہ دو لہریں بڑھی جاتی ہیں، اس کھوئے ہوئے لمحے سے
ٹکراتی ہیں، اور پھر لوٹ آتی ہیں،
کہ جیسے ایک ہچکی آئے اور پھر سانس رک جائے۔
میں کیوں کھویا ہوں رات کی گہری اداسی میں؟

مجھے گریہ سنائی دے رہا ہے،
یہی جی چاہتا ہے پاس جاکر بھی اسے سن لوں
مگر ڈر ہے جب اس کے پاس پہنچا میں تو گریہ ختم ہوگا، ایک
گہری خامشی ہوگی۔

In time's bosom—

The age is a sea with no shores,

In which tears are futile,

The sobbing shore.

I see all, I laugh and cry.

The two waves rise, crash into a lost moment, and return

As a hiccup stops the breath—

Why am I lost in night's deep sorrow?

I hear weeping,

I wish to go near and listen;

But I fear, when I reach it, it will cease and be

A deep silence.

ایک نظم

اے پیارے لوگو!

تم دور کیوں ہو؟

کچھ پاس آؤ،

آؤ کہ پل میں

یہ سب ستارے

تاریکیوں کے

اس پار ہوں گے۔

اے پیارے لوگو!

میں تم سے مل کر

بہتر بنوں گا

ایسے اکیلے

یوں روتے روتے

آنسو بہیں گے

اور کچھ نہ ہوگا

تم پاس آؤ

پھر دیکھ لیں گے

دنیا ہے کیا کچھ

اور دین کیا ہے،

پھر جان لیں گے

ہر سانس کیسے

آنکھیں جھپکتے

اَن مِٹ بنا تھا۔

Poem

Dear people!

Why so far?

Come closer

All these stars

Will be on the other side

Of darkness.

Sweet people!

Meeting you will improve me

So alone

Crying like this

Tears will flow

Nothing else will happen.

Come close

Then we'll see

What the world is

And religion.

Then we'll know

How every breath

Was made, instantly

Indelible.

لیکن   محبّت

یہ کہہ رہی ہے

ہم دُور ہی دُور

اور دُور ہی دُور

چلتے رہیں گے

سمندر کا بلاوا

یہ سرگوشیاں کہہ رہی ہیں اب آؤ کہ برسوں سے تم کو بلاتے بلاتے مرے

دل پہ گہری تھکن چھا رہی ہے

کبھی ایک پل کو کبھی ایک عرصہ صدائیں سنیں مگر یہ انوکھی ندا آرہی ہے

بلاتے بلاتے تو کوئی نہ اب تک تھکا ہے نہ آیندہ شاید تھکے گا،

"مرے پیارے بچے" ― "مجھے تم سے کتنی محبّت ہے" ― "دیکھو" اگر

یوں کیا تو

بُرا مجھ سے بڑھ کر نہ کوئی بھی ہوگا ― "خدایا، خدایا!"

کبھی ایک سسکی، کبھی اک تبسّم، کبھی صرف تیوری

مگر یہ صدائیں تو آتی رہی ہیں

انہی سے حیاتِ دوروزہ ابد سے ملی ہے

مگر یہ انوکھی ندا جس پہ گہری تھکن چھا رہی ہے

But love

Is saying

We shall continue walking

Far from one another

Farther and farther.

Call of the Sea

Sounds whisper: "Come now, come! Years of calling and calling

Have fatigued my soul."

For a moment, for an age, I have heard the voices,

Who never tire of calling.

And now comes this curious voice:

"My sweet child, how I love you, should you do this,

None would be worse than I, O Lord!"

They always come, voices, in every form,

In sobbing, smiles, or frowns.

Through them this brief life meets eternity,

But this strange voice, full of fatigue,

یہ ہر اک صدا کو مٹانے کی دھمکی دئے جا رہی ہے

اب آنکھوں میں جنبش نہ چہرے پہ کوئی تبسّم نہ تیوری
فقط کان سنتے چلے جا رہے ہیں
یہ اک گلستاں ہے ۔۔۔۔ ہوا لہلہاتی ہے، کلیاں چٹکتی ہیں،
غنچے مہکتے ہیں اور پھول کھلتے ہیں، کھل کھل کے مُرجھا کے
گرتے ہیں، اک فرشِ مخمل بناتے ہیں جس پر
مری آرزوؤں کی پریاں عجب آن سے یوں رواں ہیں
کہ جیسے گلستاں ہی اک آئینہ ہے،
اسی آئینے سے ہر اک شکل نکھری، سنور کر مٹی اور مٹ ہی گئی پھر نہ ابھری
یہ پربت ہے ۔۔۔۔ خاموش، ساکن،
کبھی کوئی چشمہ ابلتے ہوئے پوچھتا ہے کہ اس کی چٹانوں کے اس پار کیا ہے؟
مگر مجھے کو پربت کا دامن ہی کافی ہے، دامن میں وادی ہے، وادی میں ندی
ہے، ندی میں بہتی ہوئی ناؤ ہی آئینہ ہے،
اسی آئینے میں ہر اک شکل نکھری، مگر ایک ایک پل میں جو مٹنے لگی ہے تو
پھر نہ اُبھری

یہ صحرا ہے ۔۔۔۔ پھیلا ہوا، خشک، بے برگ صحرا
بگولے یہاں تند بھوتوں کا عکس مجسم بنے ہیں
مگر میں تو دُور۔۔۔۔ ایک پیڑوں کے جھرمٹ پہ اپنی نگاہیں جمائے ہوئے ہوں
نہ اب کوئی صحرا، نہ پربت، نہ کوئی گلستاں

Threatens always to drown all voices.

Now, eyes know no movement, the face wears

    neither smile nor frown,

Ears only go on listening.

Here is a rose garden: where winds ripple, buds open, blossoms

    yield fragrance, flowers bloom, fade, and fall,

    to spread a velvet floor

On which my longings move delicately, like mythical fairies,

    mirrored in the garden,

A mirror where each face appeared, settled, and dissolved forever.

The mountain is silent and still,

Though some fountain, rising, might ask what lies

    beyond those rocky peaks.

But enough for me is the mountain's foot — in whose valley

A stream carries a boat, another mirror

Where each face clearly surfaced and dissolved forever.

Here is a desert — expansive, parched, leafless,

Here whirlwinds house fierce spirits,

But I am distant — my eyes focused on a grove of trees.

Now there is no desert, mountain, or rose garden;

اب آنکھوں میں جنبش نہ چہرے پہ کوئی تبسم نہ تیوری

فقط ایک انوکھی صدا کہہ رہی ہے کہ تم کو بلاتے بلاتے مرے دل پہ
گہری تھکن چھا رہی ہے ،

بلاتے بلاتے تو کوئی نہ اب تک تھکا ہے نہ شاید تھکے گا
تو پھر یہ ندا آئینہ ہے ، فقط میں تھکا ہوں

نہ صحرا نہ پربت، نہ کوئی گلستاں، فقط اب سمندر بلاتا ہے مجھ کو
کہ ہر شے سمندر سے آئی، سمندر میں جاکر ملے گی۔

یگانگت

زمانے میں کوئی بُرائی نہیں ہے
فقط اک تسلسل کا جُھولا رواں ہے
یہ میں کہہ رہا ہوں
میں کوئی برائی نہیں ہوں، زمانہ نہیں ہوں، تسلسل کا جھولا نہیں ہوں
مجھے کیا خبر کیا برائی میں ہے ، کیا زمانے میں ہے ، اور پھر
میں تو یہ بھی کہوں گا
کہ جو شے اکیلی رہے اس کی منزل فنا ہی فنا ہے ،
بُرائی، بھلائی، زمانہ، تسلسل ۔۔۔ یہ باتیں بقا کے گھرانے سے آئی ہوئی ہیں
مجھے تو کسی بھی گھرانے سے کوئی تعلق نہیں ہے
میں ہوں ایک، اور میں اکیلا ہوں، ایک اجنبی ہوں،
یہ بستی، یہ جنگل، یہ بہتے ہوئے راستے اور دریا

In the eyes no life, on the face no smile or frown:

Merely a strange voice droning that it is exhausted through calling.

Voices always calling.

So the voice is a mirror — only I am weary.

No desert, no mountain, no rose garden,

The sea alone calls me:

All comes from the sea, all will return.

Concord

There is no mischief in the age,

Merely the oscillation of a chain.

This is what I say:

I am no mischief, or the world, or the swinging of the chain.

What do I know of evil, of the world? And I will say also,

Whatever remains alone is destined for death of self.

Evil, virtue, the world, succession—these notions come

      from the house of eternity,

And I have ties to no house.

I am one, alone, a stranger.

This dwelling, jungle, flowing path and river,

Mountain; suddenly

یہ پربت، اچانک نگاہوں میں آتی ہوئی کوئی اونچی عمارت،

یہ اُجڑے ہوئے مقبرے اور مرگِ مسلسل کی صورت مجاور،

یہ ہنستے ہوئے ننھّے بچّے، یہ گاڑی سے ٹکرا کے مرتا ہوا ایک اندھا مسافر،

ہوائیں، نباتات اور آسماں پر ادھر سے اُدھر آتے جاتے ہوئے چند بادل۔

یہ کیا ہیں؟

یہی تو زمانہ ہے، یہ ایک تسلسل کا جھولا رواں ہے

یہ میں کہہ رہا ہوں

یہ بستی، یہ جنگل، یہ رستے، یہ دریا، یہ پربت، یہ عمارت، مجاور، مسافر،

ہوائیں، نباتات اور آسماں پر ادھر سے اُدھر آتے جاتے ہوئے چند بادل،

یہ سب کچھ، یہ ہر شے مرے ہی گھرانے سے آئی ہوئی ہے،

زمانہ ہوں میں، میرے ہی دم سے ان مٹ تسلسل کا جھولا رواں ہے،

مگر مجھ میں کوئی برائی نہیں ہے

یہ کیسے کہوں میں

کہ مجھ میں فنا اور بقا دونوں آکر ملے ہیں۔

Some high building comes into view.

Desolated graves, graveyard workers ever wearing

  death's countenance;

Laughing children, a blind man dying, struck by a car;

Winds, clouds roaming all over field and sky—

What are these?

They are the world, the swinging chain of events.

Here is what I say:

Dwelling, jungle, roads, river, mountain, building,

  graveyard worker, passenger,

Winds, clouds roaming over field and sky:

All these, everything has come from my own house.

I am the world, the breath behind the indelible swinging chain,

Yet there is no mischief in me.

How shall I convey that

Death of self and resurrection

Meet

In me?

مجھے گھر یاد آتا ہے

سمٹ کر کس لئے نقطہ نہیں بنتی زمین؟ کہہ دو!

یہ پھیلا آسماں اس وقت کیوں دل لُبھاتا ہے ؟

ہر اک سمت اب انوکھے لوگ ہیں اور ان کی باتیں ہیں

کوئی دل سے پھسل جاتی کوئی سینہ میں چبھہ جاتی

انہی باتوں کی لہروں پر بہا جاتا ہے یہ بجرا

جسے ساحل نہیں ملتا

میں جس کے سامنے آؤں، مجھے لازم ہے ہلکی مسکراہٹ

میں کہیں یہ ہونٹ ''تم کو

جانتا ہوں'' دل کہے ''کب چاہتا ہوں میں''

انہی لہروں پہ بہتا ہوں مجھے ساحل نہیں ملتا

سمٹ کر کس لئے نقطہ نہیں بنتی زمین، کہہ دو

وہ کیسی مسکراہٹ تھی، بہن کی مسکراہٹ تھی، میرا
بھائی بھی ہنستا تھا

وہ ہنستا تھا، بہن ہنستی ہے اپنے دل میں کہتی ہے

یہ کیسی بات بھائی نے کہی، دیکھو وہ امّاں اور ابّا کو ہنسی آئی

مگر یوں وقت بہتا ہے تماشا بن گیا ساحل

مجھے ساحل نہیں ملتا!

سمٹ کر کس لئے نقطہ نہیں بنتی زمیں، کہہ دو

یہ کیسا پھیر ہے، تقدیر کا یہ پھیر تو شاید نہیں لیکن

یہ پھیلا آسماں اس وقت کیوں دل کو لبھاتا تھا؟

I Remember Home

Why, I ask, does the earth not shrink to a point?

Why, at first, did this wide sky lure the heart?

All around are strange people, strange words:

Some slide over the heart, others pierce it.

On these waving words flows the heart's vessel,

Which finds no shore.

Whomever I meet I duly greet, smiling, but what lips affirm

In "I know you," the heart denies with "I don't."

I move on those waves

And find no shore.

Why does this earth not shrink to a point?

What a smile, my sister's smile, my brother laughing,

She delighting in his words,

Delighting in our parents' laughter!

Yet time flows on, the shore a spectacle.

I find no shore.

Why does the earth not shrink to a point?

Perhaps this cycle lies outside of fate; why

Did this wide sky once lure the heart?

حیاتِ مختصر سب کی بھی جاتی ہے اور میں بھی

ہر اک کو دیکھتا ہوں مسکراتا ہے کہ ہنستا ہے

کوئی ہنستا نظر آئے کوئی روتا نظر آئے

میں سب کو دیکھتا ہوں، دیکھ کر خاموش رہتا ہوں

مجھے ساحل نہیں ملتا!

The brief life of all things flows on; and I

Watch each one, smiling, laughing,

Weeping.

Watching, I am silent.

I find no shore.

AKHTAR UL-IMAN

Akhtar ul-Iman (1915–) was born in Uttar Pradesh, India. He received his MA from Aligarh University and became a screenplay writer and director in the film industry. Though he was a member of the Progressive Writers' Association, his verse is individualistic in its portrayal of character and its exploration of hitherto untreated dimensions of experience in colloquial language. He tended to frown on the overt use of literature for political ends and indeed affirmed the artistic autonomy of poetry. Yet his verse sometimes portrays the devastating psychological effects of British rule and reacts against many prevailing social and religious conventions.

عَہدِ وفا

یہی شاخ تم جس کے نیچے کسی کے
لئے چشم نم ہو، یہاں اب سے کچھـ سال پہلے

مجھے ایک چھوٹی سی بچّی ملی
تھی، جسے میں نے آغوش میں لے کے پوچھا تھا، بیٹی،

یہاں کیوں کھڑی رو رہی ہو، مجھے اپنے بوسیدہ
آنچل میں پھولوں کے گہنے دکھا کر

وہ کہنے لگی میرا ساتھی، اُدھر، اُس نے انگلی
اٹھا کر بتایا، اُدھر اس طرف ہی

(جدھر اونچے محلوں کے گنبد، ملوں کی سیہ چمنیاں
آسماں کی طرف سر اٹھائے کھڑی ہیں)

یہ کہہ کر گیا ہے کہ میں سونے چاندی کے
گہنے ترے واسطے لینے جاتا ہوں رامی

FROM *Kulliyat* (Collected Works)

Vow of Faith

Here, at this very bough, beneath which

Your eyes moisten for someone,

Some years ago I chanced upon a small girl.

Sitting her on my lap, I asked, "Why, my dear, do you stand

here crying?"

She took a garland from her ragged shawl, and spoke:

"My friend, over there (pointing), where

The high palace domes and the mills' black chimneys

Stand, with heads reared toward the sky;

Over there my friend has gone. He said, 'Rami, I'll go

To bring garlands for you,

Garlands of silver and gold.'"

میرا دوست ـــــ ابُوالہَول

دھواں دھار تقریر جس نے ابھی کی تھی وہ آدمی ہے

جو لفظوں کے پُل باندھتا ہے

ابھرتے ہوئے نوجوانوں کو وعدوں کی افیون دے کر

اِسی پُل پہ لاتا ہے اور غرق کرکے

پلٹ جاتا ہے حسبِ دستور آرام گہہ کو

یہ دنیا تو ان شعلہ سامان لوگوں نے آپس میں تقسیم کرلی

جو ہتھیار کی شکل میں رنج و غم ڈھالتے ہیں

یا گولہ بارود کے کارخانوں کے مالک ہیں

یا پھر ثنا خواں ہیں اُن کے

ہمارے لئے صرف نعرے بچے ہیں

صنعتی دَور کے کج کلاہوں کی داد و دہش روح پرور ہو یا جان لیوا

مگر زندہ باد، آفریں، مرحبا کے سوا کچھہ نہیں پاس اپنے

یہ سب جانتا ہے ہماری شجاعت کی پرواز کیا ہے

ہماری جواں مردی اک صوبہ جاتی تعصّب سے ـــــ

یا فرقہ واری فسادات سے آگے کچھہ بھی نہیں ہے

فتوحاتِ اسکندری ہم نے تختی پہ لکھہ کر مٹا دی ہے کب کی

ہمارے بہادر زمیں کے تلے سو رہے ہیں

عجائب گھروں میں لٹکتی ہیں تلواریں ان کی

My Friend Abul Haul

What a fiery speech this orator made,

A bridge of words,

Feeding promises like opium to upsurging youth;

Leading them to this bridge;

Drowning them,

He returns to his high station, his easy living.

The world has been carved up by these fiery souls

Who forge weapons from misery and grief,

Who own arms factories

Or speak in their cause.

Only slogans are left for us:

The bounty of our proud industrial lords

May sustain life or destroy it,

But we have no response, only "Long may they live!,"

      "Well done!," "Bravo!"

He knows well our valor, its lofty flight!

Our manliness is but a province of bigotry:

Nothing beyond quarreling sect and faction.

Alexander's conquests we carved on tablets and erased long ago.

Beneath our brave soil our warriors lie,

Their swords hang in museums,

اور ان کے زرّیں لبادوں کو گُھن کھا گیا ہے

زرہ بکتروں پر کلونس آ گئی ہے

یہ سب جانتا ہے ہماری تگ و تاز کیا ہے

ہمارے شکم گر ہمارے سروں پر نہ ہوتے

اور چہروں میں اعضائے جنسی

تو ہم اچھّے انسان بنتے

ہمارے گھروں کے کم و بیش سب عقبی دروازے پیہم کھلے ہیں

ہمارے لہو میں ہرے لال پیلے بہت سارے پرچم گُھلے ہیں

کہیں سے مگر حق کی آواز آتی نہیں ہے

ہماری زباں دل کی ساتھی نہیں ہے

ہمارے لئے کھوکھلا لفظ جمہوریت ہے تقاریر ہیں لیڈروں کی

ہمارے لئے روزناموں کے صفحات ہیں اشتہارات ہیں نیم جنسی

ہمارے لئے دیوتاؤں کے بت ہیں خدا کے فرامین ہیں اور عقبیٰ

جو بد رنگ ہے حال کی طرح اور کورے لٹھے کی بو سے بھری ہے

ہمارے لئے صرف روٹی کی جد و جہد

عورتوں کے برہنہ بدن کی تمنّا سے آگے کہیں کچھ نہیں ہے

ہماری رگوں میں جو تیزاب ہے اس کی شدّت کبھی کم نہ ہوگی!

Decay devours their golden robes,

Rust runs through their coats of mail.

He well knows our exertions!

Were we not deformed, thinking through

Our bellies and private parts,

We'd be fine human beings.

Our back doors all stand open;

In our blood are mixed green, red, and yellow flags.

Yet the sound of truth is heard nowhere,

Our tongue is no disciple of our heart.

For us, the hollow word *democracy*, the speeches of leaders,

Newspaper columns, erotic advertisements;

For us, images of deities, God's commandments, the afterlife—

All are discolored, our own condition, full of the stench

      of unwashed cloth.

For us, the toil for bread,

A consuming craving for female flesh.

The pungent acid in our veins

Will never sweeten.

ایک لڑکا

دیار شرق کی آبادیوں کے اُونچے ٹیلوں پر
کبھی آموں کے باغوں میں کبھی کھیتوں کی مینڈوں پر
کبھی جھیلوں کے پانی میں کبھی بستی کی گلیوں میں
کبھی کچھ نیم عریاں کم سِنوں کی رنگ رلیوں میں
سحردم، جُھٹپٹے کے وقت، راتوں کے اندھیرے میں
کبھی میلوں میں، ناٹک ٹولیوں میں، ان کے ڈیرے میں
تعاقب میں کبھی گُم، تتلیوں کے سونی راہوں میں
کبھی ننّھے پرندوں کی نہفتہ خواب گاہوں میں
برہنہ پاؤں جلتی ریت یخبستہ ہواؤں میں
گریزاں بستیوں سے، مدرسوں سے، خانقاہوں میں
کبھی ہم سِن حسینوں میں بہت خوش کام و دل رفتہ
کبھی پیچاں بگولہ ساں، کبھی جیوں چشمِ خوں بستہ
ہوا میں تیرتا خوابوں میں بادل کی طرح اُڑتا
پرندوں کی طرح شاخوں میں چُھپ کر جھولتا، مُڑتا
مجھے اک لڑکا، آوارہ منش، آزاد سیلانی
مجھے اک لڑکا، جیسے تند چشموں کا، رواں پانی
نظر آتا ہے، یوں لگتا ہے، جیسے یہ بلائے جاں
مرا ہمزاد ہے، ہر گام پر، ہر موڑ پر جولاں
اسے ہمراہ پاتا ہوں، یہ سائے کی طرح میرا
تعاقب کر رہا ہے، جیسے میں مفرور ملزم ہوں
یہ مجھ سے پوچھتا ہے اختر الایمان تم ہی ہو؟

A Boy

On the high hills of homes in the eastern province,

In mango groves, on the skirts of fields,

In marsh water, in town alleys,

In the playfulness of half-naked children,

In morning's early hours, at dusk, in night's dark shadow,

In fairs, in the tents of performing bands,

Lost in pursuit, in the open tracks of butterflies,

In hidden nests where small birds rest,

Barefoot in freezing wind and burning sand,

Fleeing from towns and schools to monasteries,

Delighting in young beauties,

Like a twisting whirlwind, like an eye weeping blood,

He swims in the wind and flies like a cloud in dreams,

Like a bird, hopping and turning, hidden in branches,

A boy, a free spirit, given to wandering,

A boy, like water rushing from a gushing fountain,

Appears to me, his restless spirit appears to be

My twin spirit, present at every step, every turn,

Always with me, pursuing

Like my shadow, and I a fugitive.

He demands, Akhtar ul-Iman, is it indeed you?

خدائے عزّ و جل کی نعمتوں کا معترف ہوں میں
مجھے اقرار ہے اس نے زمیں کو ایسے پھیلایا
کہ جیسے بستر کم خواب ہو، دیباؤ مخمل ہو
مجھے اقرار ہے یہ خیمۂ افلاک کا سایا
اسی کی بخششیں ہیں، اس نے سورج چاند تاروں کو
فضاؤں میں سنوارا اک حدِ فاصل مقرّر کی
چٹانیں چیر کر دریا نکالے خاکِ اسفل سے
مری تخلیق کی مجھ کو جہاں کی پاسبانی دی
سمندر موتیوں مونگوں سے کانیں لعل و گوہر سے
ہوائیں مست کُن خوشبوؤں سے معمور کر دی ہیں
وہ حاکم قادرِ مطلق ہے، یکتا اور دانا ہے
اندھیرے کو اُجالے سے جدا کرتا ہے، خود کو میں
اگر پہچانتا ہوں اس کی رحمت اور سخاوت ہے!
اسی نے خسروی دی ہے لئیموں کو مجھے نکبت
اسی نے یاوہگویوں کو مرا خازن بنایا ہے
تونگر ہرزہکاروں کو کیا دریوزہ گر مجھ کو
مگر جب جب کسی کے سامنے دامن پسارا ہے
یہ لڑکا پوچھتا ہے اختر الایمان تم ہی ہو؟

معیشت دوسروں کے ہاتھ میں ہے میرے قبضہ میں
جز اک ذہنِ رسا کچھ بھی نہیں پھر بھی مگر مجھ کو
خروشِ عمر کے اتمام تک اک بار اٹھانا ہے

I acknowledge the blessings of divine grandeur,

I accept that He has spread the earth

Like a silken bed, of velvet and brocade;

I own that the shadow of the sky's tent

Is bestowed by Him, that He arranged the sun, moon,

And stars in space, fixing their limits,

Rending the mountains, opening up rivers from dusty depths.

He created me, gave to me the world's protection,

Filling the sea with pearl and coral, mines with ruby and jewel,

And the winds with ravishing scents.

He is the omnipotent sovereign, unique and wise,

He separates darkness and light; if I know myself,

It is through His mercy and bounty.

He has given royalty to the miserly, misfortune to me,

He has made vain talkers my treasurers,

Idlers he has made wealthy and me a beggar,

But as soon as my cloak is spread before someone,

This boy asks, are you indeed Akhtar ul-Iman?

Subsistence is in others' hands, in my control is

Nothing beyond shrewdness, yet

Until the end of my clamoring years I must carry a burden.

عناصر منتشر ہو جائے نبضیں ڈوب جائے تک
نوائے صبح ہو یا نالۂ شب کچھ بھی گانا ہے
ظفرمندوں کے آگے رزق کی تحصیل کے خاطر
کبھی اپنا ہی نغمہ ان کا کہہ کر مسکرانا ہے
وہ خامہ سوزی شب بیداریوں کا جو نتیجہ ہو
اسے اک کھوٹے سکّے کی طرح سب کو دکھانا ہے
کبھی جب سوچتا ہوں اپنے بارے میں تو کہتا ہوں
کہ تو اک آبلہ ہے جس کو آخر پھوٹ جانا ہے
غرض گرداں ہوں بادِ صبح گاہی کی طرح، لیکن
سحر کی آرزو میں شب کا دامن تھامتا ہوں جب
یہ لڑکا پوچھتا ہے اخترا لایمان تم ہی ہو؟

یہ لڑکا پوچھتا ہے جب تو میں جھلا کے کہتا ہوں
وہ آشفتہ مزاج، اندوہ پرور، اضطراب آسا
جسے تم پوچھتے رہتے ہو کب کا مر چکا ظالم
اسے خود اپنے ہاتھوں سے کفن دے کر فریبوں کا
اسی کی آرزوؤں کی لحد میں پھینک آیا ہوں!
میں اس لڑکے سے کہتا ہوں وہ شعلہ مر چکا جس نے
کبھی چاہا تھا اک خاشاکِ عالم پھونک ڈالے گا
یہ لڑکا مسکراتا ہے، یہ آہستہ سے کہتا ہے
یہ کذب و افترا ہے، جھوٹ ہے دیکھو میں زندہ ہوں!

Until the mind's elements are distracted, and the pulse fades,

I'm obliged to sing, whether morning song or nightly lamentation.

Before those who rule, I must, to earn bread,

Sing their own song to them, to make them smile;

Passionate words coined through the sleepless night

I must exhibit, like counterfeit coins, to everyone.

I say to myself, I am a blister

Bound in the end to burst.

In short, I am wandering like the morning breeze.

But I clasp the cloak of night in hope of morning, when

This boy asks, Akhtar ul-Iman, is it indeed you?

When this boy inquires, I answer in rage,

That distracted, anguished man, nourishing grief, for

Whom you keep asking, he died long ago.

With his own hands he laid the shroud over deceptions;

I have thrown his dreams into the grave!

I tell the boy, the flame has died that desired

To scorch away the rubbish of the world.

The boy smiles, saying softly,

You deceive yourself, you see,

I still live!

MAJID AMJAD

Majid Amjad (1914–74) was born in Jhung (now in Pakistan). After graduating from Islamia College, Lahore, he entered journalism, editing the weekly *Uruj*, after which he worked for the government. He lived a relatively secluded life, and his poetry focuses on intensely personal experience. One volume of his poems, *Shab-e Rafta,* was published before his death. Since then, a number of selections of his poetry and his complete works have appeared in print. Amjad belongs to the broad modernistic movement in Urdu poetry pioneered by Rashed and Miraji. His poetry tends to shy away from political involvement and instead withdraws into a highly subjective world.

فرد

اتنے کڑے وسیع نظام میں صرف ایک میری ہی نیکی سے کیا ہوتا ہے

میں تو اس سے زیادہ کر ہی کیا سکتا ہوں

میز پر اپنی ساری دنیا: کاغذ اور قلم اور ٹوٹی پھوٹی نظمیں

ساری چیزیں بڑے قرینے سے رکھ دی ہیں،

دل میں بھری ہوئی ہیں اتنی اچھی اچھی باتیں،

اُن باتوں کا دھیان آتا ہے تو یہ سانس بڑی ہی بیش بہا لگتی ہے

مجھے کو بھی تو کیسی کیسی باتوں سے راحت ملتی ہے

مجھے کو اس راہ میں صادق پاکر

سارے جھوٹ مری تصدیق کو آ جاتے ہیں

ایک اگر میں سچّا ہوتا،

میری اس دنیا میں جتنی قرینے سجے ہوئے ہیں

ان کی جگہ بے ترتیبی سے پڑے ہوئے کچھ ٹکڑے ہوتے

میرے جسم کے ٹکڑے، کالے جھوٹ کے اس چلتے آرے کے نیچے!

اتنے بڑے نظام سے میری نیکی ٹکرا سکتی تھی،

اگر اک میں ہں سچّا ہوتا!

Individual

In this order, vast and fixed, of what use is my virtue?

What can I do?

My whole world lies on my table: paper, pen, fragments of poems

All in pristine order.

Knowing the high thoughts that hold my heart,

This breath knows its worth.

What thoughts come to comfort me!

Finding me true on this path,

All lies come to vouch for me.

Were I alone true,

My world's order

Would collapse in chaos, into scattered fragments:

My broken body, sundered by black falsehood.

Against this huge order my virtue could have clashed

Were I alone true.

راتوں کو

آنکھوں میں کوئی بس جاتا ہے

میٹھی سی ہنسی ہنس جاتا ہے

احساس کی لہریں ان تاریک جزیروں سے ٹکراتی ہیں

جہاں نغمے پنکھ سنوارتے ہیں

سنگین فصیلوں کے گنبد سے پہرے دار پکارتے ہیں

"کیا کرتا ہے "

دل ڈرتا ہے

دل ڈرتا ہے، ان کالی اکیلی راتوں سے دل ڈرتا ہے

اِن سُونی تنہا راتوں میں

دل ڈوب کے گزری باتوں میں

جب سوچتا ہے، کیا دیکھتا ہے، ہر سمت دھوئیں کا بادل ہے

وادی و بیاباں جل تھل ہے

ذخّار سمندر سوکھے ہیں، پُر ہول چٹانیں پگھلی ہیں

دھرتی نے ٹوٹتے تاروں کی جلتی ہوئی لاشیں نگلی ہیں

پنہائے زماں کے سینے پر اک موج انگڑائی لیتی ہے

اس آب و گل کے دلدل میں اک چاپ سنائی دیتی ہے

اک تھرکن سی، اک دھڑکن سی، آفاق کی ڈھلوانوں میں کہیں

تانیں جو ہمک کر ملتی ہیں، چل پڑتی ہیں، رکتی ہی نہیں

In the Nights

In my eyes lives

Someone,

Laughs sweetly;

Waves of feeling lap against these dark islands

Where songs adorn their wings.

From the domes of stony city walls, guards call out:

"Who goes there?"

My heart shivers,

Fears

The black of these deserted nights.

In these desolate nights

When, sunk in memory, the heart thinks back, it sees

Smoke billowing on every side,

Valley and desert flooded,

Rough seas run dry, mighty rocks melted,

Earth embracing falling stars like flaming corpses,

A wave stretching across time's hidden heart.

In these marshes, a footstep sounds

Like a beat, a rhythm, somewhere on the horizon's slopes:

Notes that embrace and join, never ceasing;

ان راگنیوں کے بھنور، بھنور میں صدہا صدیاں گھوم گئیں

اس قرن آلود مسافت میں لاکھ آبلے پھوٹے، دیپ بُجھے

اور آج کسے معلوم ضمیرِ ہستی کا آہنگِ تپاں

کس دُور کے دیس کے کہروں میں لرزاں لرزاں، رقصاں رقصاں

اس سانس کی رو تک پہنچا ہے

اس میرے میز کی جلتی ہوئی قندیل کی لو تک پہنچا ہے

کون آیا ہے؟ کون آتا ہے؟ کون آئے گا؟

انجانے من کی مُورکھتا کو کیا کیا دھیان گزرتا ہے

دل ڈرتا ہے،

دل ڈرتا ہے ان کالی اکیلی راتوں سے دل ڈرتا ہے!

In the whirlpool of these ragas have spun centuries.

In this age-deep journey, wounds have erupted in thousands,

      lamps have died.

And now, who knows through the mists of what far lands

Human conscience in its restless melody, shaking, gyrating,

Has danced to reach the rhythm of my breath

And the flaming lamp on my desk?

Who has come? Who is coming? Who will come?

Who knows what thoughts journey through a strange heart?

My heart trembles,

Fears

These lonely nights, black.

MUNIR NIAZI

Munir Niazi (1928–) is usually thought of as an imagist poet. Born in Hoshiapur, India, he attended Dayal Singh College in Lahore and worked for Pakistan television. He also did freelance writing and composed film songs. He published several volumes of poetry. Like Majid Amjad, he follows in the modernistic tradition of Rashed and Miraji, expressing intensely personal states of mind and feeling.

دیکھنے والے کی الجھن

سُورج میں جو چہرے دیکھے

اب ہیں سپنے سمان

اور شُعاعوں میں الجھی سی

گیلے گیلے ہونٹوں کی وہ لال نئی مسکان

جیسے کبھی نہ زندہ تھے یہ

چھوٹی چھوٹی اینٹوں والے ٹھنڈے برف مکان

کہاں گئی وہ شام ڈھلے کی

سرسر کرتی تیز ہوا کی دل پر کھنچی کمان

اور سپنا جو نیند میں لایا

پوری ادھوری خواہشوں کا

اک درد بھرا طوفان

کوئی کیسے کرسکتا ہے ان سب میں پہچان

سائے

کسی سائے کا نقش گہرا نہیں ہے

ہراک سایہ اک آنکھ ہے

جس میں عشرت کدوں، نارسا خواہشوں

ان کہی دلنشین داستانوں کا میلہ لگا ہے

مگر آنکھ کا سحر، پلکوں کی چلمن کی ہلکی سی جنبش

اور کچھ نہیں ہے

An Onlooker's Confusion

Faces I have seen in the sun

Seem now like dreams,

And moist lips with their young red smile,

Entrapped in rays, as though

They had never breathed;

Icy cold houses of small brick.

Where, as evening falls, has gone the bow

Of the hissing wind, stretched over the heart,

And the dream that unleashed in sleep

The pain, the storm

Of desires fulfilled and unfulfilled?

Who could distinguish them?

Shadows

No shadow makes a deep impression;

Every shadow is an eye

Hosting a carnival of

Pleasure houses, vain desires, enthralling stories all untold.

The magic of the eyes

Is nothing,

کسی آنکھ کا سحر دائم نہیں ہے

ہر اک سایہ
چلتی ہوا کا پُر اسرار جھونکا ہے
جو دور کی بات سے
دل کو بے چین کرکے چلا جائے گا
ہر کوئی جانتا ہے
ہواؤں کی باتیں کبھی دیر تک رہنے والی نہیں ہیں
کسی آنکھ کا سحر دائم نہیں ہے
کسی سائے کا نقش گہرا نہیں ہے

خوبصورت زندگی ہم نے کیسے گذاری

آج کا دن کیسے گذرا ہے، کل گذرے گا کیسے
کل جو پریشانی میں بیتا وہ بھولے گا کیسے
کتنے دن ہم اور جئیں گے، کام ہیں کتنے باقی
کتنے دکھ ہم کاٹ چکے ہیں، اور ہیں کتنے باقی
خاص طرح کی سوچ تھی جس میں سیدھی بات گنوا دی
چھوٹے چھوٹے وہموں ہی میں ساری عمر بتا دی

A flutter of eyelashes,

Every eye's magic dies.

Every shadow

Is a mystery, waving upon the wind

To fuel the heart's impatience

With talk of fancies, before it

Flies.

The wind's speech fades,

The eye's magic dies,

The shadow's trace is always gone.

How I Passed a Beautiful Life

How today has gone, how tomorrow shall,

How shall yesterday, passed in grief, be gone from mind;

What days are left for me, what tasks remain

What sorrows have passed, what remain;

Lost in obscure thought, I lost truth:

My years squandered in small cares, illusion.

SAQI FAROOQI

Saqi Farooqi (1936–) was born in Gorakhpur, India. His family migrated to Bangladesh and then Karachi. He moved to London, where he still lives. He has published several volumes of poetry, including one book in English, as well as a substantial volume of literary criticism. Though he is a great admirer of N. M. Rashed, his poetry has a highly distinctive, direct, and sometimes explosive voice. It is remarkable for its compressed and powerful imagery. He experiments with rhyme, meter, and neologisms in his persistently controversial challenges to conventional thinking and feeling.

حاجی بھائی پانی والا

دونوں مَشکیزے لَبالَب

ایک چُمبک کی طرح

اپنی جانب کھینچتے رہتے اُسے

فیل بندی قہر تھی ——

مرد گاہک مسخری کرتے ہوئے ڈرتے

ذرا محتاط رہتے

جُھرجُھری کا سوانگ بھرتے ——

عورتیں مغموم آنکھوں میں

تَرس کاڑھے ہوئے

اپنے بچوں پر بَرس پڑتیں

اگر وہ بدلحاظ

بھولپن سے پوچھ لیتے :

"کیوں نہیں،

اُسکے فلانوں کی طرح

اِنکے فلانے کیوں نہیں" ——

FROM *Haji-Bhai, Pani-Wallah*

Haji-Bhai, Pani-Wallah

Both skin bags overflowing,

Pulling him earthward

Like a magnet:

A punishment,

A bishop under pawn control.

His male customers joke but fear,

Are cautious,

Seeming to shiver—

Women, their sad eyes

Brimming with pity,

Shower fury on their children

For asking innocently,

"Why are our balls small, Mummy!

Not like his!!"

"Haji" refers to someone who has undertaken the hajj (pilgrimage to Mecca). "Pani-Wallah" literally means a person who carries water; in this case, the phrase refers metaphorically to the disease of hydrocele suffered by the persona (the haji) of this poem. The entire phrase "Haji-Bhai, Pani-Wallah" is an epithet attached to a proper name. Such a naming practice is common in some of the village communities of Pakistan. In this poem the epithet is used in place of the proper name.

وہ خدائی فرش پر اکڑوں،

کبھی گوتم کے آسن میں، کبھی

تہمد سے باہر پاؤں پھیلاکے،

اکڑ کر بیٹھتا ____

بار بار اس واسطے پہلو بدلتا ____

____جَگلری¹ کرتا کہ پیروں میں

ہمیشہ جَھنجَھنی کے جُھنجُھنے بجتے

عجب اک مستقل سی بے کَلی رہتی ____

وہ غبّارے پھٹے پڑتے تھے

جن پر تانت سی نیلی رگیں پھولی ہوئی

نَنھے مُنّے کیچووں کی طرح

کنڈلی مار کے بیٹھی ہوئی تھیں ____

جس طرح گھینگا چُھپانے کے لئے

اپنے سر سیّد کی داڑھی ...

ہو بہو

پلپلے تربوز پر

اس کی لُنگی میز پوش ایسی پڑی رہتی ____

اس مَرض کا فائدہ اتنا ہُوا

اَپنی چَوکی سے فراغت پا گیا

Jugglery¹

Squatting on God's earth

Sometimes in the posture of Buddha, sometimes with

His feet spread outside his loincloth,

He sits, cramped.

Ever changing position,

He juggles, feet alive

With tingling and jingling,

A totally restless wonder.

Like balloons ready to burst

On which lean blue veins had swollen

Like tiny worms

Sitting coiled—

As if, to hide his water sac

With his Sir Syed beard . . .¹

On the feeble watermelon

His loincloth outspread like a tablecloth—

In his disease was one bonus:

He found freedom from his stool.

---

¹The reformer Sir Sayyad Ahmad Khan wore a beard, which happened to hide swollen glands in his throat.

یہ کہ ردّی پھاڑ کر

اپنے تھیلے اپنی گودی میں سمیٹ

وہ اِنھی پر

ساری پڑیائیں بناتا

لَونگ، دَھنیا، دارچینی، جائے پھل اور تیج پات

سب مسالے اس کی رانوں کے مزے

چکھّے ہوئے تھے ——

غِیبتی جَل ککڑے ایسے تھے کہ بس

صاف کہتے اس نے کعبے کی زیارت ہی

نہیں کی ہے

فقط اجمیر جاکر لَوٹ آیا

بلکہ یہ بھی مشتَبَہ

اس پہاڑی سے اترنا

دوسری کا قصد کرنا

حاجیوں کی دھینگا مُشتی، لپّا ڈُگّی، ریل پیل

Tearing scrap paper,

Gathering his bags in his lap,

He would prepare right there

All his pouches

Of clove, cinnamon, nutmeg, bay leaves;

Spices all enriched by the taste

Of his thighs.

Some folk, prone to backbiting,

Would plainly declare that he'd never

Made the pilgrimage to Mecca,[2]

That he'd only been to Ajmir;[3]

Even this, they'd say, was doubtful.

To descend one mountain,

To attempt another,[4]

The jostling, crowding bustle of pilgrims;

---

[2]A Muslim is required to make pilgrimage to Mecca once in a life-time. Mecca was the birthplace of Muhammad, the holy prophet of Islam.

[3]A city in northern India that houses the tomb of the Muslim saint Moin-uddin Chishti

[4]Among the rituals performed during the pilgrimage is the act of running between the hill of Safa and the hill of Marwa in com-memoration of the desperate search for water in the desert under-taken by Hajar, wife of Abraham.

پھر گناہوں کے پٹارے کی طرح لَٹلکی ہوئی

فالتو گٹھری الگ

اس کی حالت غیر تھی

حج تو ممکن ہی نہیں ———

جتنے حاسد اتنی باتیں

ایک روز

وہ اُلہنوں سے نِڈھال

موت کی بانہوں میں بانہیں ڈال کے

اپنے آقا کی طرف

اپنے راز اپنے "مفاعیلن" اُٹھائے چل پڑا ———

کسی مُلک میں ایک تھا بادشا ———

——— ہمارا تمہارا خدا بادشا[2]

---

[2]چونکہ "بادشاہ" حرمزدگی کرتے رہتے ہیں اس لئے میں نے
ان کے ہجے بدل دئے ہیں. ساقی

Hanging, like baskets of sin

His own useless bundles:

In his unique condition

Hajj was hardly possible—

As many rumors as backbiters!

One day

Run down from reproaches

Hand in hand with death,

Toward his God,

Taking his secrets,

His sacred mountains, he went—

The King is dead,[5]

Long live the King . . .

---

[5]A traditional formula for ending a story

حَمل سَرا

دادی امّاں.............
(بستی کے سب سے ممتاز
گھرانے کی بیٹی ....
سب سے معزّز
آنگن کی دلہن ....
ماشا اللہ
ستّر کے پیٹے میں ہونگی)
.... اپنا استحقاق مانگتی ہیں

دادا جان کہ
دس کم ساٹھ برس تک ان سے
اندھی گھپ کالی راتوں میں
چھپ چھپ کے ملنے آئے
بیوی کی زرخیز آنکھوں میں
صرف اولادِ نرینہ کے
خواب اگا کے چلے گئے——

یہ شوہر کے رستے میں
حائل نہ ہوئیں
دل کے ٹکڑے
ہوسٹلوں میں پلے بڑھے
حیف کہ اُن کے دکھ سکھ میں
شامل نہ ہوئیں

Womb Palace

Grandma . . .

Daughter of the city's noblest kin . . .

Bride of the most honored court,[1]

Praise be to God,

She, in her seventies

. . . demands her right.

Grandfather

For sixty years

In the pitch-black nights

Would come in stealth to see her

Only to plant, in his wife's fertile eyes

The dream of a son—

She would never stand

In the path of her husband's will;

Her children reared in hostels,

She was aloof from

Their sorrows, their joys.

The title adapts the Urdu phrase *mahal-sera*, which means "palace."
[1]Or "family"

دادا جان کی سخت طبیعت نے

اِس کا موقع ہی نہ دیا

یہ وہ ناطق

جو خاموش رہیں ——

اُس نازیبا خاموشی میں

آگ لگانے کے دن آئے

اب اپنے چَقمَاق مانگتی ہیں ——

ان کے اندر تنہائی کا زہر اُترتا چلا گیا

(اور زمانہ

ارد گرد سے

پرچھائیں کی طرح گزرتا چلاگیا)

سوگ میں ہیں،

تریاق مانگتی ہیں ——

ایک جنم تک

اندھی گونگی بہری بن کے

اپنے ہی گھر میں بے دخل،

بے قدری کے "سخی حسن" میں دفن رہیں

آج نئے آفاق مانگتی ہیں

دادی امّاں طلاق مانگتی ہیں ——

Grandfather's stern nature

Would not have it;

She was a soul, endowed with speech

Who kept silence—

In this unbecoming silence

Came the day to light a fire:

Now

She demands her flint—

Inside her, loneliness descended like poison

(All-enveloping Time

Merely passed, vanishing like a shadow).

She suffers,

She demands

An opiate.

Existing, a whole cycle of life

As if blind, dumb, deaf,

Exiled in her own house,

Entombed in worthlessness.

Today she craves new horizons:

She demands

A divorce.

FAHMIDAH RIAZ

Fahmidah Riaz (1946–) was born in Uttar Pradesh, India. She graduated from Sind University and undertook film studies in London. During the rule of martial law in Pakistan under Zia ul-Haq, she was arrested in 1977 and charged with sedition for her editing of the controversial magazine *Awaaz* and with treason for her views on the coexistence of Bangladesh and India. She took refuge in India, not returning to Pakistan until Zia ul-Haq's regime was terminated. When Benazir was ousted, Riaz was declared persona non grata. After Benazir's reelection, Riaz worked at the Ministry of Culture until Benazir was again deposed. Riaz's poetry is outspoken in its treatment of women. She defies religious norms and gender roles in her determination to reach into the depths of sensuous experience. She continues to give poetry readings at international forums. She lives in Karachi.

باکرہ

آسماں تپتے ہُوئے لوہے کی مانند سفید
ریگ سُوکھی ہوئی پیاسے کی زباں کے مانند
پیاس حلقوم میں ہے، جسم میں ہے، جان میں ہے

سر بزانو ہوں، جھلستے ہُوئے ریگستاں میں
تیری سرکار میں لے آئی ہُوں یہ وحش ذبیح!
مجھ پہ لازم تھی جو قربانی وہ مَیں نے کر دی

اس کی اُبلی ہُوئی آنکھوں میں ابھی تک ہے چمک
اور سیہ بال میں بھیگے ہُوئے خوں سے اب تک
تیرا فرمان یہ تھا اس پہ کوئی داغ نہ ہو
سو یہ بے عیب اچھوتا بھی تھا ان دیکھا بھی
بے کراں ریگ میں سب گرم لہُو جذب ہُوا
دیکھ چادر پہ مری ثبت ہے اس کا دھبّا
اے خُداوند کبیر
اے جبّار!
متکبّر و جلیل!
ہاں ترے نام پڑھے اور کِیا ذبح اسے
اب کوئی پارۂ ابر آئے، کہیں سایہ ہو
اے خُداوند عظیم

FROM *Badan Daridah*
(Torn Body)

Virgin

A sky white like incandescent iron,

Sand dried up like a parched tongue,

Thirst torments throat, body, soul.

My head bowed on my lap in this scorching desert.

In your service I have brought this slaughtered beast;

I have performed the due sacrifice.

There is still a glimmer in its bulging eyes,

Its black hair still drenched with blood.

Your command was that it should bear no blemish,

Hence this faultless creature was untouched, unseen.

Boundless sand soaks up all the warm blood:

See, on the sheet is my mark, its stain:

O great God!

The almighty!

Proud and August!

Reciting your name, I sacrificed it.

Now may some cloud descend, some shade from somewhere

O high God,

بادِ تسکیں! کہ نفس آگ بنا جاتا ہے!

قطرۂ آب کہ جاں لب پہ چلی آئی ہے

لاؤ، ہاتھ اپنا لاؤ ذرا

لاؤ، ہاتھ اپنا لاؤ ذرا

چھوکے میرا بدن

اپنے بچّے کے دل کا دھڑکنا سنو

ناف کے اس طرف

اس کی جنبش کو محسوس کرتے ہو تم؟

بس یہیں چھوڑ دو

تھوڑی دیر اور اس ہاتھ کو میرے ٹھنڈے بدن پر یہیں چھوڑ دو

میرے بے کل نفس کو قرار آ گیا

میرے عیسیٰ! مرے درد کے چارہ گر

میرا ہر موئے تن

اس ہتھیلی سے تسکین پانے لگا

اس ہتھیلی کے نیچے مرا لال کروٹ سی لینے لگا

انگلیوں سے بدن اس کا پہچان لو

تم اسے جان لو

چومنے دو مجھے اپنی یہ انگلیاں

اُن کی ہر پور کو چومنے دو مجھے

ناخنوں کو لبوں سے لگا لوں ذرا

Some soothing winds! For my spirit is fire;

A drop of water! For my life hovers near the verge.

Come, Bring Your Hand Here

Come, bring your hand here,

Feel my body,

Hear the beating of your child.

Do you feel its movement

On this side of the navel?

Stop—leave your hand here,

Let it rest a little longer here on my cold body.

Peace has come to my wild spirit,

My Christ! Healer of my pain!

Every hair of my body

Feels comfort from the palm of your hand;

Beneath this palm my child begins to turn:

Recognize his body with your fingers,

Know him.

Let me kiss these fingers,

Let me kiss their every joint,

Let me press your nails to my lips,

اس ہتھیلی میں منہ تو چھپا لوں ذرا

پھُول لاتی ہوئی یہ ہری انگلیاں

میری آنکھوں سے آنسو ابلتے ہُوئے

ان سے سینچوں گی مَیں

پھُول لاتی ہوئی انگلیوں کی جڑیں۔ چومنے دو مجھے

اپنے بال، اپنے ماتھے کا چاند، اپنے لب

یہ چمکتی ہوئی کالی آنکھیں

مرے کانپتے ہونٹ، میری چھلکتی ہُوئی آنکھ کو
دیکھ کر کتنی حیران ہیں

تم کو معلوم کیا ۔ تم کو معلوم کیا

تم نے جانے مجھے کیا سے کیا کر دیا

میرے اندر اندھیرے کا آسیب تھا۔

یا کراں تا کراں ایک انمٹ خلا

یوں ہی پھرتی تھی مَیں

زیست کے ذائقے کو ترستی ہوئی

دل میں آنسُو بھرے، سب پہ ہنستی ہُوئی

تم نے اندر میرا اس طرح بھر دیا

پھُوٹتی ہے مرے جسم سے روشنی

Let me hide my face in your palm,

These green fingers bearing flowers;

With tears swelling in my eyes

Let me kiss the prints of your fingers bearing flowers.

Let me kiss your hair, the crescent of your forehead, your lip.

How surprised are

Those glittering black eyes,

Those smiling bemused eyes

On seeing my

Trembling lips, my overflowing eyes

What do you know of all this?

What do you know of what you have done

To me?

There was a ghost of darkness inside me:

A vacuum stretching from end to end;

I would roam about

Yearning to relish life,

Teary eyed, laughing at everything.

You have filled the vacuum inside me:

Light explodes from my body.

سب مقدّس کتابیں جو نازل ہوئیں

سب پیمبر جو اب تک اتارے گئے

سب فرشتے کہ میں بادلوں سے پرے

رنگ، سنگیت، سُر، پھول، کلیاں، شجر

صبحدم پیڑ کی جھومتی ڈالیاں

ان کے مفہوم جو بھی بتائے گئے

خاک پر بسنے والے بشر کو مسرّت کے جتنے بھی نغمے سنائے گئے

سب رشی، سب مُنی، انبیا، اولیا

خیر کے دیوتا، حُسن، نیکی، خُدا۔۔۔۔۔

آج سب پر مجھے

اعتبار آ گیا، اعتبار آ گیا

آڈن کے نام

یہ سچ ہے مِرے فلسفی

میرے شاعر

وہ وقت آ گیا ہے

کہ دنیا کے بوڑھے فریبی معلّم کا جُبّہ پکڑ کر

نئے لوگ کہہ دیں

کتابیں بدل دو!

یہ جُھوٹی کتابیں

All the scriptures which have descended,

All the prophets so far sent down,

All the angels beyond the clouds,

Colors, songs, melodies, flowers, buds, branches,

The swinging boughs of trees at daybreak:

All their meanings which have been shown,

All the sung delights of mortal creatures,

All saints, holy men, prophets,

The gods of well-being, beauty, purity, God:

In all these

I have come to have faith—faith.

To Auden

It's true, my philosopher,

My poet,

The time has come for

New people

To seize the robes of the world's old, false teachers,

To shout:

Change your books!

False books

جو ہم کو پڑھاتے چلے آ رہے ہیں

حقیقت کے رُخ سے

یہ بے معنی، فرسودہ لفظوں کے پردے ہٹا دو

جلا دو

کتابیں جو ہم نے پڑھی ہیں

جلا دو

کتابیں جو کہتی ہیں دُنیا میں حق جیتتا ہے

یہ سب کذب و بیہودہ گوئی مٹا دو

یہ سب کُچھ غلط ہے

کہ ہم جانتے ہیں

کہ جُھوٹ اور سچ میں ہمیشہ ہوئی جنگ

اور

جُھوٹ جیتا ہے

کہ نفرت امر ہے

کہ طاقت ہے برحق

کہ سچ ہارتا ہے

کہ شیطان نیکی کے احمق خُدا سے بڑا ہے

Which come to teach us.

Tear away these veils,

These meaningless, worn words

From Truth's face.

Burn them!

The books we've read!

Which claim the world is ruled by Truth.

Abolish this absurd falsehood:

We know

That Truth and Falsehood have ever warred,

That Falsehood has won,

And hatred lives immortal.

We know

That force is right,

That Satan is

Greater than the foolish

God of purity.

کب تک

کب تک مُجھ سے پیار کروگے

کب تک؟

جب تک میرے رحم سے بچّے کی تخلیق کا خُون بہے گا

جب تک میرا رنگ ہے تازہ

جب تک میرا انگ تنا ہے

پر اس سے آگے بھی تو کُچھ ہے

وہ سب کیا ہے

کِسے پتہ ہے

وہیں کی ایک مسافر مَیں بھی

انجانے کا شوق بڑا ہے

پر تم میرے ساتھ نہ ہوگے تب تک

Until When

Until when will you love me,

When?

Until child-creating blood seeps from my womb;

As long as my color is fresh,

My body firm.

Yet there is somewhere beyond this:

I too have traveled from there.

I long for the unknown realm:

You won't be with me until then.

پتّھر کی زبان

اسی اکیلے پہاڑ پر تُو مجھے ملا تھا

یہی بلندی ہے وصل تیرا

یہی ہے پتّھر مری وفا کا

اجاڑ، چٹیل، اداس، ویراں

مگر میں صدیوں سے، اس سے لپٹی ہوئی کھڑی ہوں

پھٹی ہوئی اوڑھنی میں سانسیں تری سمیٹے

ہوا کے وحشی بہاؤ پر اڑ رہا ہے دامن

سنبھالا لیتی ہوں پتھروں کو گلے لگا کر

نکیلے پتّھر

جو وقت کے ساتھ میرے سینے میں اتنی گہرے اتر گئے ہیں

کہ میرے جیتے لہو سے سب آس پاس رنگین ہو گیا ہے

مگر میں صدیوں سے اس سے لپٹی ہوئی کھڑی ہوں

اور ایک اونچی اڑان والے پرند کے ہاتھ

تجھے کو پیغام بھیجتی ہوں

تو آکے دیکھے

تو کتنا خوش ہو

کہ سنگریزے تمام یاقوت بن گئے ہیں

دمک رہے ہیں

گلاب پتّھر سے اگ رہا ہے!

FROM *Patthar ki Zaban*
(**Tongue of Stone**)

Tongue of Stone

On this lonely mountain I met you;

This height is your union,

This, the stone of my fidelity,

Desolate, bleak, sad, wilderness.

But for centuries I have stood embracing this.

Your breath gathers in my torn scarf,

My dress flies on the wind's wild breath,

I balance myself embracing stones,

Sharp pointed stones

Which through time have pierced me deep,

So my blood fills with color everything around.

But for centuries I have stood embracing this,

And I am sending a message to you

With a bird winging high:

If you come, you'll rejoice to see

All the pebbles have turned to garnets

Glowing,

A rose is growing from the stone!

پچھتاوا

خدائے ہر دو جہاں نے جب آدمی کو پہلے پہل سزا دی

بہشت سے جب اسے نکالا

تو اس کو بخشا گیا یہ ساتھی

یہ ایسا ساتھی ہے جو ہمیشہ ہی آدمی کے قریں رہا ہے

تمام ادوار چھان ڈالو

روایتوں میں، حکایتوں میں

ازل سے تاریخ کہہ رہی ہے

کہ آدمی کی جبیں ہمیشہ ندامتوں سے عرق رہی ہے

وہ وقت جب سے کہ آدمی نے

خدا کی جنت میں شجر ممنوعہ چکھ لیا

اور

سرکشی کی

تبھی سے اس پھل کا یہ کسیلا سا ذائقہ

آدمی کے کام و دہن میں ہر پھر کے آ رہا ہے

ـــــ مگر ندامت کے تلخ سے ذائقے سے پہلے

گناہ کی بے پناہ لذّت!!

Remorse

In the beginning, when first

The Lord of the two worlds

Punished Man;

When he threw him from Paradise

Granting him his mate,

His eternal friend;

Search the ages,

Through tradition and tales,

From time's beginning, history says,

Man's forehead is wet with the sweat of remorse.

Since he tasted

That tree,

Rebelling;

Since then

That bitter taste

Wells up in his mouth

Again and again.

But before remorse, before its bitter taste set in,

What unguarded pleasure in sin!

سورۂ یاسین

یہ آخرِ شب کا سنّاٹا!

اس نیم اندھیرے رستے پر

جلدی میں قدم بڑھاتی ہوئی

مَیں ایک اکیلی عورت ہوں

بڑی دیر سے میرے تعاقب میں

اِک چاپ ہے جو چلی آتی ہے

گھر ـــــ!

میرا گھر ـــــ!

مَیں اپنے گھر کیسے پہنچوں

سوکھے حلقوم اور بیٹھتے دل سے سوچتی ہوں

شاید مَیں رستہ بُھول گئی

یہ راہ تو میری راہ نہیں

اس راہ سے مَیں کب گزری تھی

سب گلیوں پر یہاں نام لکھے

اس گلی پہ کوئی نام نہیں

اور دُور دُور تک دَم سادھے

یہ سارے گھر انجانے ہیں

لو پیلے چاند کا ٹکڑا بھی

Sura Ya Sin

Night's lifeless silence:

On a road half steeped in darkness

Walking quickly,

I am alone, a woman,

Footsteps long

Pursuing me.

Home . . . !

My home . . . !

How will I reach home?

Throat choked, heart sinking, I wonder

If I've lost my way:

This street is not my street,

When did I ever pass this street?

All the neighboring streets have names;

This has none.

And, as if holding their breath, the houses all around

Seem unfamiliar.

Look, a sliver of yellow moon

The title of the poem is the title of a chapter in the Qur'an. It comprises abbreviated Arabic letters; it is not known for what they stand. Some scholars regard them as a mystic title of Muhammad, the holy prophet of Islam.

کالے پتوں میں ڈُوب گیا

اب کُچھـ بھی نہیں

بس میرے مُنہ میں خوف سے بھاری اور مفلوج زباں ہے

یا

تلووؤں سے اُوپر چڑھتی ہوئی

میرے انگ انگ میں رچی ہُوئی

اِک خنکی ہے

Sinks beneath black leaves.

Now there is nothing.

In my mouth is a tongue heavy with fear, unmovable.

I walk on tiptoe:

Through every part of my body sinks

Coldness.

KISHWAR NAHEED

Kishwar Naheed (1940–) was born in Uttar Pradesh. She graduated from Panjab University, in Lahore, and assumed a number of distinguished cultural positions such as editing the journal *Mah-e Nau* and chairing the Pakistan Arts Council. She has maintained an active theoretical as well as poetic interest in feminism: not only has she translated Simone de Beauvoir's *The Second Sex* but she has also written her own speculative work, *Aurat: Khwab aur Khak ke Darmian* (1995; Woman: Between Dream and Dust), on the status of women in feudal society. Naheed lives in Islamabad. Her poetry tends to be direct, experiential, and critical of conventional male assumptions about women.

آگہی

پلے تھے ہم کوٹھڑی کے اندر

کہ جس کی دیوار ٹیڑھی ہوکے

ہزار کونوں میں بٹ چُکی تھی

کہ جس کی کڑیاں ہماری ماں کی کمر کی صُورت جُھکی ہوئی تھیں

کہ جس کا دروازہ، تیل سرسوں کا پی کے کُھلتا تھا، بند ہوتا تھا

اور کواڑ جس کے، ہزار چھیدوں کا آئینہ تھے

مگر وہی کوٹھڑی

جہاں پہ ہوا گزرنے کا راستہ بھی کوئی نہیں تھا

ہماری بالیدگی کا منبع بنی

ہماری ماں نے ہمیشہ روٹی پکائی ایسے

کہ ایک تھا پیٹ میں تو اک

گود میں ہُمکتا

مگر نہ حرفِ گراں کبھی اس کے لب پہ آیا

میں آپ ماں ہوں

مگر مرے لختِ جاں کو،

آیا کی گود کی گرمیوں نے پالا

FROM *Be Nam Musafat*
(**Nameless Space**)

Insight

We grew up inside a cabin

Whose crooked walls were carved

Into a thousand angles;

Whose rafters bent low, like

My mother's back;

Whose door would hardly open or close

Without sesame oil;

And whose gates mirrored a thousand openings.

Yet that cabin,

Too small even to house the wind,

Housed our growth.

Our mother would bake bread, one child

In her stomach, one lounging in her lap.

No complaint fell from her lips.

I myself am a mother,

But my darling ones

Were nurtured in the warmth of a nurse's lap.

مجھے تو آرام ہے، کہ ہر روز مُنہ اندھیرے

وہ سامنے والی بیکری سے

منگالوں مَیں ناشتہ جو چاہوں

پلک جھپکنے میں، جاکے بازر سے خریدوں

جو چیز چاہوں

مجھے خبر ہے

اگر یونہی، میری ماں کی صورت

مری کمر بھی جُھکی تو کوئی نہ ساتھ دے گا

نہ مامتا کے مزار پر فاتحہ پڑے گا

غرض کے بندھن ہیں سارے رشتے

نہ مامتا نہ دلار کُچھ ہے

نہ تیرا میرا ہی پیار کُچھ ہے۔

عکس نما

ہم وہ معصوم تھے

جن کے لیے اِلہام ہر اک فقرہ تھا

ہر چمکتا ہُوا چہرہ تھا خُدا

ہر مہکتا ہُوا دامن، فردوس

ہر نظر گوشۂ امید و خبر

ہر قدم مژدۂ تمہیدِ جزا

ہم نے جب آنکھ کی تحریر کو پڑھنا سیکھا

ہر چمکتے ہُوئے چہرے کی جبلّت ڈھونڈی

My life is easy, ordering

Breakfast from the bakery, all my needs

From the bazaar.

I know

If, like my mother's, my back were bent

No one would help,

No one would recite prayers at the shrine of a mother's love.

All relations are bound by interest:

A mother's love and affection are nothing;

Your love and my love is

Nothing.

Reflection Appearing

We were the naive ones

For whom every phrase was revelation,

Every shining face was God,

Every scented garment paradise,

Every sight housed hope and novelty,

Every step foreboded the time of reckoning.

Learning the language of eyes,

We sought the essence of every bright face;

ہر مہکتے ہوئے دامن کو پکڑنا چاہا
ہر نئے نقش سے قسمت کو سمجھنا چاہا
جذبِ موہوم تھا افشار گلو
شوق زنجیر تھا
امید سزا تھی اپنی
چاہتیں دام تھیں
آہٹ بھی صدا تھی اپنی
لب نہ ہلتے تھے
نہ آنکھوں کے دیے جلتے تھے
لمحے سہمے ہوئے، چپ چاپ گُزر جاتے تھے
نقشِ محبوب ابو الہَول نظر آتے تھے

اب تو فرخندہ جفاکار ہیں ہم
اب تو پڑھ لیتے ہیں ہر سادہ ورق کی تحریر
اب نہیں کرتے وفا کی تقصیر
اب ہر اک شخص سے ملتے ہیں بدل کر شکلیں
اپنے قابو میں ہیں اب فتنۂ شب کی سوچیں
اب ہمیں خوفِ ہلاکت بھی نہیں
اب کوئی آئینہ، معیار عدالت بھی نہیں

We wished to grasp every scented garment,

To divine the stratagems of fate in each new picture:

These imagined feelings hung, a chain

Around my neck.

Zeal was a chain,

Hope, our punishment,

Desire, a snare.

Footsteps echoed our own voice,

Lips did not move,

Nor did eyes shine.

The moments would pass in fear, in silence.

A lover's image would seem like abu al haul.

Now we are happy tyrants:

We read the writing, plain, on each page.

Now we don't commit the crime of faith.

We meet each person with altered countenance.

In our dreams roam thoughts of evil nights;

Now we fear not even death.

No mirror is the measure of justice.

آگ اور برف کے درمیان آنکھیں

یورپ کے شہر برف تلے دبے ہیں

اور مرا دل بھی

سُنا ہے وہاں کے لوگ ٹرینوں میں

پھنسے رہ گئے

تو اخبار کی سرخیاں بنیں

ہم کہ یہاں بے جہت رواں ہیں

اور نہیں جانتے کہ کہاں جانا ہے

ہماری خبریں اخباروں میں کیوں نہیں آتی ہیں

مُردوں کی آنکھیں زندہ لوگوں کی بینائی تو بن رہی ہے

مگر زندہ لوگوں کی زندہ آنکھیں کیا دیکھ رہی ہیں

سچ کو جھوٹ کی میزان میں تُلتے

کہ شہروں کو امن کے نام پر

لاشوں سے پٹتے

یقین کرو بارش نہیں ہوگی

رحمت میرے رب کی

خبیث لوگوں کے لیے نہیں ہے

Eyes between Fire and Snow

Europe's cities are buried under snow,

My heart also.

There, I hear, people

Trapped in trains

Make newspaper headlines;

Here, we live to no purpose,

Blindly moving:

Do newspapers speak of us?

The living see through the eyes of the dead,

But what do the eyes of the living see?

Truth weighed in the scales of falsehood,

Corpse-filled cities proclaiming peace.

No rain will come:

The Lord's mercy

Is not for the wicked.

تیسرے درجے والوں کی پہلی ضرورت

بولنا ہماری ضرورت ہے

چاہے، زمین میں منہ دے کر ہی کیوں نہ بولنا پڑے

میری بے گنہی زمین میں منہ دے کر

اپنی صفائی پیش کر رہی ہے

کہ زندگی کے سارے راستوں پر

قاضیٔ شہر کے فیصلے کے مطابق

خوف بچھایا جا چکا ہے

بولنے والے ہمارے شہر میں کتنے رہ گئے ہیں

ان کے سر کاٹ کر واقعی سجا لینے چاہئیں

کہ پھر دیکھنے کو بھی ایسے لوگ نہیں ملیں گے

خدا کی قسم

میری آنکھوں کی جگہ آبلے بھی لے لیں

تو بھی میں گریہ نہیں کروں گی

کہ میرے کھیتوں میں چیخیں اگ رہی ہیں

میرے آنگنوں میں ٹھہری خاموشی

میرے بچّوں کی ہنسی لُوٹ رہی ہے

میرا چپڑاسی وردی پہننے سے انکار کرتا ہے

کہ وردیاں تیسرے درجے کے شہری کی علامت بن چکی ہیں

بات تو علامت سے بھی آگے نکل چکی ہے

چھپکلی کی کٹی ہوئی دم کی علامت ہو کہ

بوئے خُوں کی علامت

The First Need of Third-Class People

Our need is to speak

Even with our faces to the ground.

My innocence, face to the ground,

Proves itself.

For on all roads

Fear has been spread,

Answering to the city's judge;

How many speaking people are left in our city?

If their severed heads were used as ornaments,

You would never see such people.

By God,

Even if blisters replace my eyes,

I will not complain

That my fields are full of screams;

That silence in my courtyards

Freezes my children's laughter;

That my house attendant refuses a uniform,

A sign, he says, of a third-class citizen.

At stake is more than symbolism,

Whether the symbol of a lizard's chopped tail

Or the symbol of the smell of blood.

اب سب خوف کے دوسرے نام ہیں

ہم لوگوں کو اپنے ہی وطن میں جلا وطن کر دیا گیا ہے

کہ ہم بے روح جاندار، قصدِ گویائی سے بھی محروم ہیں

زوالِ استحصال

یہ ہاتھ جن میں رگیں اُبھر کے

خزاں کی آمد کی نامہ بر ہیں

رگیں، کبھی یُوں تپش زدہ تھیں

کہ جیسے سیّال آگ

بے آب مچھلیوں کی طرح ہو بے کل

یہ ہاتھ اٹھے نہیں دُعا کو

یہ ہاتھ، دستِ طلب کی صُورت

کہیں سبک سر نہیں ہوئے ہیں

یہ ہاتھ اپنی ہی آرزووٗں کے

قاتل و ناخُدا رہے ہیں

یہ ہاتھ کہ جن کی اُنگلیوں میں

مشقّتوں کے عذاب نے

ہر گِرہ کو چِپٹا بنا دیا ہے

ہر ایک ناخن، شکستہ ساحل کی شکل میں

Now, these are names for fear:

We have been exiled in our own country,

As soulless animals, deprived even of trying

To speak.

Declining Exploitation

These hands with protruding veins

Are messengers of approaching autumn;

The veins would burn

Like liquid fire,

Restless, like waterless

Fish.

These hands were never raised in prayer;

These hands were never cheap, begging;

These hands, the murderers and captains

 Of their own desires;

These hands whose finger joints

Tormenting toil

Has worn out,

Every nail an empty shore,

بد نمائی کا آئینہ بنا ہے

یہ میرے اچھّے دِنوں کی تصویر ابتدا ہے

A mirror of ugliness.

This is the beginning

Of my good days.

Akbar Hyderabadi

Akbar Hyderabadi (1925–) was born in Hyderabad, India, where he started writing poetry at an early age. After studying architecture in Bombay, he migrated to England in 1955, where he has remained active in the Urdu literary scene. He has published four volumes of poetry. Much of his verse has a romantic quality that in his later work is blended with more modern attitudes derived from poets such as Faiz and Rashed.

نیلسن منڈیلا کی ڈائری کے دو ورق

(۱) رہائی سے پہلے

کہتے ہیں، زنداں کے تالے ٹوٹنے والے ہیں

کہتے ہیں، برسوں کے قیدی

چھوٹنے والے ہیں

لیکن میرے روزنامچے کے اَوراق

آج بھی دھندلے   آج بھی کالے ہیں!

شاہراہ پہ ارض وطن کی

آج بھی کچھ دَھرتی کے لال

لَہو لہان پڑے ہیں

احتجاج کے حق کا حاصل

آج بھی کوڑے ہیں!

جتنے جَتن تم چاہو کرلو

وہ دن آنے والا ہے

کوکھ سے جب اس دَھرتی کی

وہ لاوا ابلنے والا ہے

جو سارے بیداد گروں

شدّادوں کو فرعونوں کو

پَل میں بھسم کر ڈالے گا!

FROM *Zarron se Sitaron tak*
(From Atoms to the Stars)

Two Pages from the Diary of Nelson Mandela

(I) Before Freedom

They say the fetters are about to break,

They say that long-jailed prisoners

Will feel freedom;

But the pages of my diary

Are still misty today, still black.

On the streets of my country

Are still sons of the soil,

Soiled with blood:

Protest is still not free,

It still brings flogging.

Tyrannize as you will:

I see a day

When lava, erupting from

Earth's womb, will

Scorch without warning

The Pharoahs, the "divine" rulers.

آج بہت مغموم ہوں مَیں...

اور غم سے دل ہے مَیلا

زخموں سے چھلنی ہے سینہ

نیلسن منڈیلا!

ابھی میں اپنے کنجِ قفس سے کیسے باہر آؤں؟

ایسی رہائی سے بہتر ہے

زنداں میں مر جاؤں!

(۲) رہائی کے بعد

ستائیس برس کا کہرہ

چَھٹ گیا آج فضاؤں سے

جاگ اٹھی ہیں نئی اُمنگیں

دل میں تازہ ہَواؤں سے

خوشی کے نعرے گونج رہے ہیں

میرے وطن کی گلیوں میں

رنگ اور خوشبو کی لہریں ہیں شاخ شاخ پر کلیوں میں

جیسے زمیں کا چپّہ چپّہ

گوشۂ خُلدِ بریں ہے

خاکِ وطن کا ذرّہ ذرّہ

ماہتاب جبیں ہے

آج جنوبی افریقہ پر ایک جہاں کی نظریں ہیں

Today, Nelson Mandela,

I am oppressed,

Tormented by wounds, my heart torn.

How can I walk free?

Better to die imprisoned

Than live such ugly freedom.

(II) After Freedom

The dust of twenty-seven years

Has leveled to open space;

New breezes, new longings move

In my heart.

Happy slogans echo

In the streets;

Nature's brilliance breathes again,

In waves of color and fragrance,

In buds and leaves,

As if every inch of soil

Knew the promise of paradise.

Every speck of this nation's earth

Glows, like the moon's brow.

Today, the world holds in its eyes

مجھ پر میرے قبیلے کے
ہر پیرو جَواں کی نظریں ہیں

وہ کہتے ہیں: "میز پر آؤ
مفاہمت کی بات کرو
پھینک دو اپنی تیغ و سِپر اور مصالحت کی بات کرو"

اپنے اصول کی چوکھٹ پر مَیں
کِتنی خوشیاں وار آیا
عمر عزیز کا سرمایہ بھی زندانوں میں ہار آیا
آج بھی اس دَھرتی کے جیالے
چلتی پھرتی لاشیں ہیں!
آج بھی اِس اندھے قانون سے اُن کی وہی پَرخاشیں ہیں
نیک دلی کا دعویٰ ہے تو
جور و ستم سے باز آؤ
مصالحت تو بعد میں ہوگی
پہلے کچھ کر دِکھلاؤ!

اگر وہی ہے طور تمہارا—— وہی ہماری بربادی
ترک کریں گے ہم نہ نہ اَبد تک
اپنی جنگِ آزادی!!

South Africa.

All the young and old of my tribe

Look to me.

"Come to the table,"

Say the rulers,

"Lay down your arms, and let us

Talk!"

At the threshold of integrity

I left behind ease and joy;

Prison darkness was my life.

Today our brave people are still

Walking corpses,

Still clashing with your blind laws.

Let your tyranny dissolve,

Then will come dialogue!

While your strategies remain, our suffering remains,

Our war remains.

Modern Language Association of America
Texts and Translations

Texts

Anna Banti. *"La signorina" e altri racconti.* Ed. and introd. Carol Lazzaro-Weis. 2001.

Bekenntnisse einer Giftmischerin, von ihr selbst geschrieben. Ed. and introd. Raleigh Whitinger and Diana Spokiene. 2009.

Adolphe Belot. *Mademoiselle Giraud, ma femme.* Ed and introd. Christopher Rivers. 2002.

Dovid Bergelson. אָפּגאַנג. Ed. and introd. Joseph Sherman. 1999.

Elsa Bernstein. *Dämmerung: Schauspiel in fünf Akten.* Ed. and introd. Susanne Kord. 2003.

Edith Bruck. *Lettera alla madre.* Ed. and introd. Gabriella Romani. 2006.

Isabelle de Charrière. *Lettres de Mistriss Henley publiées par son amie.* Ed. Joan Hinde Stewart and Philip Stewart. 1993.

Isabelle de Charrière. *Trois femmes: Nouvelle de l'Abbé de la Tour.* Ed. and introd. Emma Rooksby. 2007.

François-Timoléon de Choisy, Marie-Jeanne L'Héritier, and Charles Perrault. *Histoire de la Marquise-Marquis de Banneville.* Ed. Joan DeJean. 2004.

Sophie Cottin. *Claire d'Albe.* Ed. and introd. Margaret Cohen. 2002.

Marceline Desbordes-Valmore. *Sarah.* Ed. Deborah Jenson and Doris Y. Kadish. 2008.

Claire de Duras. *Ourika.* Ed. Joan DeJean. Introd. DeJean and Margaret Waller. 1994.

Şeyh Galip. *Hüsn ü Aşk.* Ed. and introd. Victoria Rowe Holbrook. 2005.

Françoise de Graffigny. *Lettres d'une Péruvienne.* Introd. Joan DeJean and Nancy K. Miller. 1993.

Sofya Kovalevskaya. Нигилистка. Ed. and introd. Natasha Kolchevska. 2001.

Thérèse Kuoh-Moukoury. *Rencontres essentielles.* Introd. Cheryl Toman. 2002.

Juan José Millás. *"Trastornos de carácter" y otros cuentos.* Introd. Pepa Anastasio. 2007.

Emilia Pardo Bazán. *"El encaje roto" y otros cuentos.* Ed. and introd. Joyce Tolliver. 1996.

Rachilde. *Monsieur Vénus: Roman matérialiste.* Ed. and introd. Melanie Hawthorne and Liz Constable. 2004.

Marie Riccoboni. *Histoire d'Ernestine*. Ed. Joan Hinde Stewart and Philip Stewart. 1998.

Eleonore Thon. *Adelheit von Rastenberg*. Ed. and introd. Karin A. Wurst. 1996.

Translations

Anna Banti. *"The Signorina" and Other Stories*. Trans. Martha King and Carol Lazzaro-Weis. 2001.

Adolphe Belot. *Mademoiselle Giraud, My Wife*. Trans. Christopher Rivers. 2002.

Dovid Bergelson. *Descent*. Trans. Joseph Sherman. 1999.

Elsa Bernstein. *Twilight: A Drama in Five Acts*. Trans. Susanne Kord. 2003.

Edith Bruck. *Letter to My Mother*. Trans. Brenda Webster with Gabriella Romani. 2006.

Isabelle de Charrière. *Letters of Mistress Henley Published by Her Friend*. Trans. Philip Stewart and Jean Vaché. 1993.

Isabelle de Charrière. *Three Women: A Novel by the Abbé de la Tour*. Trans. Emma Rooksby. 2007.

François-Timoléon de Choisy, Marie-Jeanne L'Héritier, and Charles Perrault. *The Story of the Marquise-Marquis de Banneville*. Trans. Steven Rendall. 2004.

Confessions of a Poisoner, Written by Herself. Trans. Raleigh Whitinger and Diana Spokiene. 2009.

Sophie Cottin. *Claire d'Albe*. Trans. Margaret Cohen. 2002.

Marceline Desbordes-Valmore. *Sarah*. Trans. Deborah Jenson and Doris Y. Kadish. 2008.

Claire de Duras. *Ourika*. Trans. John Fowles. 1994.

Şeyh Galip. *Beauty and Love*. Trans. Victoria Rowe Holbrook. 2005.

Françoise de Graffigny. *Letters from a Peruvian Woman*. Trans. David Kornacker. 1993.

Sofya Kovalevskaya. *Nihilist Girl*. Trans. Natasha Kolchevska with Mary Zirin. 2001.

Thérèse Kuoh-Moukoury. *Essential Encounters*. Trans. Cheryl Toman. 2002.

Juan José Millás. *"Personality Disorders" and Other Stories*. Trans. Gregory B. Kaplan. 2007.

Emilia Pardo Bazán. *"Torn Lace" and Other Stories*. Trans. María Cristina Urruela. 1996.

Rachilde. *Monsieur Vénus: A Materialist Novel*. Trans. Melanie Hawthorne. 2004.

Marie Riccoboni. *The Story of Ernestine*. Trans. Joan Hinde Stewart and Philip Stewart. 1998.

Eleonore Thon. *Adelheit von Rastenberg*. Trans. George F. Peters. 1996.

Texts and Translations in One-Volume Anthologies

Modern Italian Poetry. Ed. and trans. Ned Condini. Introd. Dana Renga. 2009.

Modern Urdu Poetry. Ed., introd., and trans. M. A. R. Habib. 2003.

Nineteenth-Century Women's Poetry from France. Ed. Gretchen Schultz. Trans. Anne Atik, Michael Bishop, Mary Ann Caws, Melanie Hawthorne, Rosemary Lloyd, J. S. A. Lowe, Laurence Porter, Christopher Rivers, Schultz, Patricia Terry, and Rosanna Warren. 2008.

Nineteenth-Century Women's Poetry from Spain. Ed. Anna-Marie Aldaz. Introd. Susan Kirkpatrick. Trans. Aldaz and W. Robert Walker. 2008.

Spanish American Modernismo. Ed. Kelly Washbourne. Trans. Washbourne with Sergio Waisman. 2007.